WHEN HALF IS WHOLE

WHEN HALF IS WHOLE

My Recovery from Stroke

Lorna Hewson

COLLINS DOVE
Melbourne Australia

Published by Collins Dove
25–37 Huntingdale Road
Burwood, Victoria 3125

© Copyright 1986 Lorna Hewson
All rights reserved. Except where allowed under Australian copyright law, no part of this book may be reproduced without permission in writing from the publishers.

Illustrations by Elaine Thurlow
Typeset by Bookset, North Melbourne
Printed in Australia by Globe Press Pty Ltd

First published 1983
Reprinted 1983, 1986
This editon 1990

National Library of Australia Cataloguing-in-Publication data

Hewson, Lorna, 1919–
   When half is whole.

   2nd ed.
   Bibliography.
   ISBN 0 85924 478 4.

     1. Hewson, Lorna, 1919– — Health. 2. Cerebrovascular disease — Patients — Australia — Biography. 3. Cerebrovascular disease — Patients — Rehabilitation — Australia. I. Title. (Series: Health and well-being series).

362.1'9681'00924

Contents

Foreword
Preface
Poem: What is it doing there?
Life-force flowing out of me ... 3
Looking for my arm ... 13
Horror trip between two hospitals ... 23
We don't use wheelchairs here 25
Home again ... 41
An outpatient ... 49
A little surprise ... 61
Rebuilding a life ... 63
Sexuality and the stroke victim ... 69
Yoga ... 77
Fine tuning ... 87
One small step ... 91
Afterword: From the other side of the blanket ... 98
Postscript ... 101
Stroke Class ... 103
Stroke Recovery Centres ... 105

Foreword

When Lorna Hewson suffered a stroke she lost the use of the left side of her body. As well, her image of herself was damaged so that she was no longer aware that there was a left side to her body or, indeed, a left side to the world about her.

A creative, gregarious, independent person, she now became introspective, fearful and dependent.

Through her work she already had some insight into problems that patients must face after having a stroke and this, combined with her own clear recall, has provided a vivid documentation of her sense of bewilderment and frustration.

In this book she recounts her sharply remembered experiences and reactions to the situation and to other people, especially the hospital staff.

The book broadens our understanding of this particular problem and is valuable reading for all people concerned with management of strokes—families, doctors, nurses and students alike.

Kevin Grant, M.B., B.S., B.Sc. (Med.),
F.R.C.P. (Edin.), F.R.A.C.P.

Preface

This updated edition of *When Half is Whole* has been generated by the flood of letters and telephone calls in response both to the book and to the spontaneous media publicity at the time of its publication. This feedback has made me acutely aware of problems and of whole areas and resources in the field of stroke medicine I had not previously considered. It also gave credibility to my personal experience of stroke. I began to realise I was becoming a resource centre in myself, that the kind of information I was receiving was apparently not available elsewhere and that there was a vast need for it to be disseminated.

Another and more personal reason for updating is that at the time I wrote *When Half is Whole* there were experiences during the time of my stroke that I was not able to talk about. These were painful episodes both in the course of the disease and in the course of the treatment afforded me as a person.

I was astounded by not only the quantity of response to the first edition, but by the far reaching impact of it, even to such a remote place as Borneo. I have heard from universities and organisations in New Zealand, England, India, Japan and the USA, as well as from all over Australia. It has opened doors I never dreamed of. Through an interpreter I have spoken to ethnic groups about stroke. I have talked to doctors, nurses, medical students, therapists, schools of nursing and allied health professionals and all kinds of groups associated with the stroke process. I have spoken on T.V. and radio, been the guest of Stroke Awareness Week, been asked to attend seminars, presented a paper at a Regional Annual Gerontology Conference, and have been instrumental in organising a Regional stroke group.

When Half is Whole was published in November 1982, it sold out before Christmas, and was reprinted in February 1983. The first avalanche of response had somewhat abated when it was reactivated by the presentation to me, at the end of September 1983, of the Bowater-Scott Award for that year. I was nominated by a nurse, unknown to me, from the Ovens and Murray Hospital in Victoria, who had attended just one of my lectures. This Award 'seeks to acknowledge women who, through their own actions, have achieved extraordinary personal goals'. A delightful surprise was a by-product of this Award. I received a bronze sculpture by Michael Meszaros, which was to me a vivid representation of the potential of the stroke patient rising out of a prone figure.

When I was asked to revise *When Half is Whole* I was, and still am, in the process of writing a second volume, to be called *Stroke: A Family Affair*. This is an attempt to address insights about the family of the stroke patient that I have gained from those who have written to me who are not patients themselves. The statement made by my husband, Ray, that 'We have had a stroke' has been shown to be poignantly true.

My hope is that my new book will help to improve the quality of relationships between patients, their families and hospital staff.

The poem that introduces this edition of *When Half is Whole* was considered and rejected as too frightening for publication in the first edition. However, I have had repeated requests for copies, from people who say it 'brings the whole (experience) into focus'.

Lorna Hewson

Poem: What is it doing there?

What is it doing there
That arm beside me on the chair?
I seem to know its shape and size
It must be my dear friend's I surmise.
Why did she leave it here with me?
Where will I put it when I go to tea?

There's a leg leaning there. Whose can it be?
I think the top part belongs to me,
The other part I've seen before
I'm puzzled as my gaze rests on the floor.
The top part is mine. The bottom is not.
I don't seem to know what I've got.

I wish someone would help me to understand
A little more about their goals and plan.
Why is an arm and leg left for me to mind?
Were they left by someone who hoped to help me find
A way to use them. What shall I do?
How can I fit the leg into my shoe?

When did I last look this way?
Was it a week, a month or a day?
My eyes water as I stare
Into a space that wasn't there.
I'm glad the space is back again,
For weeks and weeks it's been just pain.

If that leg and arm were really mine
I'd use them and I'd learn to climb
A mountain trail or a wave tossed shore
And gather shells as I had done before.
It was a 'stroke' that changed my life
Clipped the wings of a bird in flight.

Now that years have passed away
I look back and remember that awesome day
When what was mine did not appear to be
And how I felt that it belonged to thee.
I needed information then that with knowledge I may gain
The concept of myself in space
And start to live again.

by Lorna Hewson
author of *When Half is Whole*

Life-force flowing out of me

You have suffered a stroke.

Your entire body is still there in its complete physical form. But now you are aware of only *part* of your body. You have lost the feelings, sensations and messages previously sent to your brain from that half of your body of which you are now unaware.

That *other half* of your body in which you still have feeling, sensation—and hence awareness—now seems your whole body. Thus, *half is whole*.

I want to tell you my story. I could well be sitting in some corner of a nursing home, classed as 'not retrainable'. Fortunately, I was working in a hospital when my stroke occurred. This hospital offered rehabilitation training to people who had suffered strokes. For a number of years I had worked as a technical assistant in the Occupational Therapy Department of this large hospital. It was in August 1976, at the age of 56, that I suffered what is commonly called a stroke. It was then that I began to understand what it was like on the other side of the blanket—the patient's side. My stroke was caused by a cerebral haemorrhage in the non-dominant hemisphere of the brain. As a result of this, I was paralysed down the left side of my body.

When I first arrived at the Occupational Therapy Department on the day of my stroke, there were the usual greetings from the staff: 'Hello; how are you?' I remember remarking that I was tired and not quite well. The real trouble seemed to elude me. On the drive to work that morning the crackling of the car radio had irritated me, and my husband, Ray, had turned it off. He remarked that our new colour television set had caused me the same irritation on the previous night.

The morning's therapy began. I worked with a man who had suffered a stroke some months before. He was then returning to the Occupational Therapy Department three days a week to further his rehabilitation. It was at 11.30 that morning that the wood lathe in our department was switched on and a patient began working with a piece of wood. The excessively high pitched screech of metal on wood seemed to bore deep inside my head. I was in agonising pain; half an hour later, I had a stroke.

I can only describe the moment of stroke as a feeling of the life-force flowing out of the left side of my body. It was a warm, tingling sensation like the tide going out and not coming back in again. The deep pain in my head also ebbed away, but at the same time movement was becoming frozen. I kept opening and closing my left hand, trying to hold onto the movement. Then there was no movement at all. I knew that I'd had a stroke.

A doctor was summoned. He came very quickly and confirmed what I already knew.

The doctor asked me if I had any pins and needles in my left arm and chest. I answered in the affirmative and he then suspected that I may also have had a heart attack. It was a few minutes later when I was being lifted on to the trolley taking me to the Emergency Ward that I became aware of my immobility and a feeling of being attached to a heavy weight. I was shattered at my helplessness. The change was so sudden: from an active independent person to a completely dependent one. My thought was: if it were my destiny to have a stroke, why did it have to be now? I still had so much that I wanted to do. Of course there is never a right time to have a stroke.

I had always felt I was pretty much in control of my life. I had felt the whiplash of a sometimes cruel fate, but never before had I felt the devastation of immobility and utter dependence on others. In the past, if I had been in a situation that I couldn't tolerate, I had been able to walk away from it. I had always been able to make a choice. There had always been an alternative. Although other people may have influenced me in the directions I took in life, the final decision had always been mine. Suddenly in a split second, I was powerless. I couldn't walk away from this frightful experience. I was dependent on others for my very existence. Although all of these thoughts were going on in my mind, outwardly I was unable to show emotion.

During the next few hours I was in a life-threatening situation. I was rushed to the Emergency Ward. My blood pressure was constantly checked. Strangely, my body temperature did not register on the thermometer. A cardiograph was taken; it revealed that there had been no heart attack. My husband Ray arrived, closely followed by our family. It was so reassuring to see them. I don't recall any panic or pain in this initial stage. I remember seeing the tears rolling down my daughter-in-law's cheeks and feeling glad that she cared. Quite unemotionally I wondered what my prognosis was.

Immediately after my stroke I was completely unaware of anything to my left. Looking to the right was to my mind 'opposite'. There was no kind man in the bed opposite me, for in fact his bed was 'beside' mine—on the right side. In the Emergency Ward beds are on one side only. My mind was receiving false and inaccurate information about the space around me.

Another memory which remains with me from my short stay in the Emergency Ward is of an elderly gentleman who was in the bed opposite me. We could just see each other through a chink in the curtain that had been pulled around my bed. This kind man assured me that if I needed a nurse in a hurry he would ring his buzzer and summon her for me. The staff in this busy situation were coming and going all the time, but he remained in one spot. His gaze never left my face. Bless him. He made me feel so secure. Already I had lost my identity. I felt I was 'just another stroke'. This feeling is somehow tied in with the loss of ability of movement and loss of independence.

I don't remember being moved that evening on the trolley from the Emergency Ward to a four-bed medical ward. I only remember the feeling of an enormous weight attached to me as I was lifted from the trolley to the bed.

The cerebral haemorrhage had paralysed my left side (i.e. the haemorrhage was centred in the non-dominant parietal lobe of my brain which controls the messages to the left side of my body). I was therefore not aware that my left side was still there, nor aware of the world around me on my left.

My placement in the medical ward with my good right side facing the wall isolated me from the happening world of visitors and nurses and all the activities of a busy ward. This was quite devastating. Fortunately, this mistake was picked up very quickly by one of the occupational therapy staff and was rectified. However, the moving of my bed from one side of the ward to the other took place while I was asleep. When I awoke and saw all the activity of the ward which I now viewed from my aware right side, I thought I had been moved to another ward or another hospital. I was worried. Would my doctor, my husband and family be able to find me? Everyone assured me that I was in the same ward but in my mind I knew I was not. I had been the only person in the ward, I thought; there had been only the wall with a window in it, and me. The nurses who had been there when my bed was moved had now gone off duty and the new staff, even if unaware that my bed had been moved, certainly knew that I was in the same ward. They assured me that this was so, but they obviously knew nothing of my unawareness of anything on my left, including the left side of my body.

In brief, I was aware of only the right side of my body and to me that half was now the whole of my being. I felt completely lost and thought people were lying to me when they insisted I was in the same ward. I wanted to find out.

My mind seemed to separate from my body and travelled through the corridors outside the ward, examining the left hand side which had not impressed itself upon my consciousness as I was wheeled into the ward. My mind had to satisfy itself that I was in the same hospital and ward which, previously, I had known so well.

I clearly remember this experience. I became both the observer and the observed. My mind 'saw' such details as the light switches on the wall as it retraced my movement. I do not recall any weight or confusion of body image when I was in this 'free' state, but when I (my mind) returned to my body, the weight returned once more.

With my head fallen to one side and my chin on my chest, copious pillows behind me, I stared at a spot low down on the wall. I knew I was not communicating. I was too tired to talk. I was intensely aware of all that happened and all that was said, but only on my right side. My right side was my world. There was nothing else. I felt 'lost in space' and so very lonely.

I felt drained of life and movement. My eyes could not scan. I couldn't smile because I didn't know how to move the muscles of my face. At that time I had no interest in why this was so. I had no inclination to find out how to smile. I just lived from moment to moment—completely in the present, unconcerned about past or future. Pain had become my ever constant companion. I was very tired and found visitors exhausting. People standing beside my bed and talking seemed to deprive me of air. My husband Ray sat and held my hand. He was literally holding on to me. Holding my life in his hands. I could feel tremendous energy coming from him. It became very apparent to me that some people give energy. They are the givers of this world. Other people take the energy from you; disastrous when you have none to spare.

When I was wheeled to the toilet and seated on it, my heavy left leg would fall against my good leg. This distressed me because I could not pass urine. It seemed an impossible situation. It was not until a very aware nurse saw my predicament and parted my knees that I was able to relieve the intolerable pressure. I was unable to do this for myself, but thereafter asked to be positioned in this manner. My bowel movement posed another problem. It was not until the sixteenth day after my stroke that I was relieved of this discomfort by manual removal of the impacted faeces. This had to be done on seven successive occasions.

Everything seemed very still within me, but in my mind I was attached to the pain and heaviness I felt. I could not understand why. My mind asked 'Why don't they relieve the pain and heaviness? They try to lift me when I am still attached to it, and I am so heavy and such a burden'.

I couldn't locate the pain, but I had always thought that medication for the relief of pain was prescribed for patients in this intolerable situation. Mild analgesics did nothing to relieve my pain. I was unable to think or perceive anything without the intrusion of the ever-present pain. I could only cope with one thought, sound or situation at a time. My doctor had told me that he was unable to prescribe stronger medication until the cause of my stroke had been determined. I was not to receive this help until I was transferred to the Rehabilitation Unit four weeks after my stroke. Could alternative methods have been tried? I think so. Relaxation programmes are frequently used to relieve tension in mind and body, and reduce pain. Acupuncture, acupressure and massage at the back of the neck and between the shoulders is relaxing, and also a pleasant experience.

Pain formed a barrier between me and the instructions being given to me by the staff. The whole retraining program I knew so well from the occupational therapy point of view had been going round and round in my mind from the moment I had my stroke. For some years I had been using this retraining method myself to help stroke victims regain as much independence as possible. God knows I knew the program well enough. I was dismayed that I knew all the many techniques, but couldn't carry out any of them in my own situation.

Trying to locate the source of my pain, I would ask myself: 'Why don't I know where the pain is? It is severe pain and yet I can't say where it is. People who have pain and can't say where it is are thought to be crazy. Am I crazy? I am so tired, but the pain won't let me sleep.'

Here is a typical experience from those early days of pain, and confusion:

Once more my mind separates from my body. I am suddenly free but down a dark well. I try to climb the walls of the well, but they are slippery and covered with green slime. My fingers can't get a hold. I am trying to reach a small point of light. It is so bright but so far away at the top of the well. I know that if I can reach it there will be no more pain but I slip back again, and I seem to hear the words: 'Ding, dong, dell; Pussy's in the well'. Then, in the far, far distance I can hear a faint voice. I slowly open my eyes and I am back with the weight and the pain again. I find my husband is by my side to comfort me. I keep the experience of being in the well to myself. Would others understand its meaning to me?

People who are not disabled are constantly transferring their weight from one side of the body to the other, to enable them to stay in balanced, comfortable positions. This not only makes them feel secure, but reduces the stress on muscles and joints. As a patient with 'loss of body-image' I was dependent on other people to correct my posture. I needed to find a way to support my head so that it was not always in the same position: fallen to one side and therefore causing wry neck and more pain. My weakened joints should have been protected and my arm supported so that my shoulder did not become dislocated. Had the staff recognised the problem of my loss of body image and had they been aware of the effects of this loss, they would have known that I was entirely dependent on them.

And yet at the sisters' station there was a copy of a newly published booklet called 'The Newcastle Method of Management of Hemiplegia'. It was published and distributed to wards and departments in the hospital concerned with stroke. I know, I helped distribute them. I remember listening to two nurses discuss how and where it would be best to position my arm and leg when lying on my affected side. I remember telling them about the book. I think they thought I was 'raving'. I remember telling a doctor that there should be one of these booklets hanging over the end of the bed of all stroke patients. He knew what booklet I referred to as he replied, 'It would be too costly'. This valuable booklet can be purchased for the minimal price of $1.50. What price patient care.

Correct positioning is important to prevent bodily dysfunction resulting in physical complications, mental anguish and still more pain. I found there was almost no knowledge about positioning me on my hemiplegic side. On one occasion a nurse placed me in a position that was reasonably comfortable, but I was unable to recapture the position or to describe to anyone else how it was done. I now know that this lack of descriptive ability concerned my left side which lacked a definite image in my consciousness.

I was not aware that my left side was still there. I did not know of my loss. No one helped me to understand why my responses to instructions were inadequate and inappropriate. I felt as though I had lost my mind, because I couldn't comprehend what I thought should have been easily understandable to me. From babyhood my body had been sending messages to my brain, saying that my body was there, saying exactly where it was in space, and keeping me aware of the amount of space it occupied. I was not aware of these constant messages between body and brain. Try to become aware of this process yourself; you will find it is a hidden process.

Suddenly, at the moment of my stroke, this process was altered. The left side of my body stopped sending messages about itself to my brain. I did not know that this had happened, and nobody explained it to me. I needed insight into my problem and could not begin to make progress without being aware of my loss.

I felt attached to weight and pain. If I caught sight of my left arm or leg, it wasn't mine because it didn't tell me so. I didn't notice the left in any case, because the left side of me wasn't there. The real world was all to my right.

My centre of gravity had seemingly shifted to the right. The nursing staff were really very patient and were forever repositioning me at my many requests. I would be comfortable for only a few seconds, then I would slip out of the position they had put me into. I could not regain a comfortable position. How do you correct your balance or adjust your position when your image of yourself is in only half the space that you really

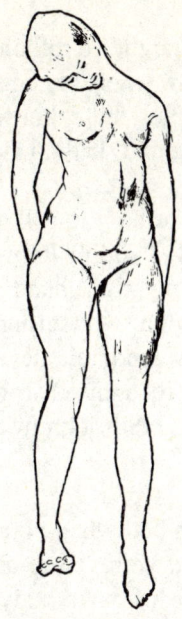 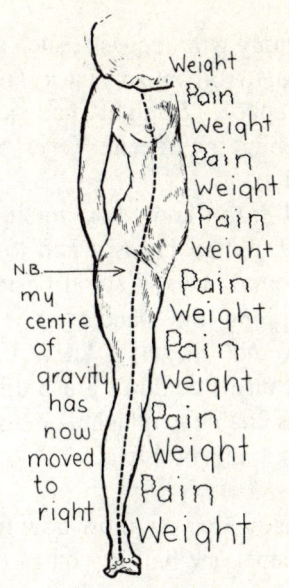

As other people saw me
The other people—family, friends, wardmaids, the paper boy, even the health professionals—saw me as a whole person, taking up the amount of space that my whole body occupied. These were the people who were caring for me and giving me instructions. They saw me in one space concept. Nobody understood my loss of body image.

As I saw myself
I felt a whole person but I didn't know that my brain was receiving messages from the right side of my body only. This represented only half my body in space. I thought of myself as a whole person, not half a person. It was impossible for me to carry out accurately instructions given to me by people who saw me in a totally different space concept.

---

occupy? It is necessary to know where the centre of your body is in order to find your balance. My concept of the line of equilibrium would have been the centre of the body that I knew about—that is, the centre of my right side. To perform tasks and comply with requests, such as to sit up straight, to roll onto my side, to roll onto my back, I needed to know where my body was in space. 'Straight' had no meaning. Nor did I know what 'behind me' meant. 'Over' and 'move around' had no meaning to me.

I didn't know how to sit up straight, or how to roll over in bed. When I was asked to turn around, I didn't know what 'around' was. I stood beside my bed, my right hand tightly gripping the handle of a wooden pylon wondering what 'around' meant. I knew I should know and felt devastated because I couldn't grasp this concept. I recognised words but was unable to attach them to movements. I didn't know how to tackle this problem.

How do you know how to roll over in bed when your mind accepts one half of you as the whole and your centre of equilibrium as the middle of the right side of your body? The mental (intellectual) and physical aspects of me were not meshing. They functioned separately—not together.

Sitting in a chair was quite intolerable. Not being able to find the centre of my body caused me so much discomfort and pain. Even though the staff went to no end of trouble in trying different chairs, my left side kept dragging me over, and I could do nothing to stop it. Remember, I didn't realise *why* I was being dragged over to my left.

Looking for my arm

'What are you doing, Lorna? Are you looking for your arm?'

When a member of the occupational therapy staff asked this question, I thought, 'My God, she thinks I have loss of body-image. She's crazy. I can feel all of me. I am whole'.

After a number of similar experiences, such as: 'Lift up so I can put a bedpan under you', you lift up what you think is all of you, only to hear the nurse say, 'The other side, too'. You think you have lifted *all* of you . . . the *all* of you *that you know about,* but you don't know that you have loss of body-image. Is it any wonder you start to feel stupid?

I now realise that the occupational therapist who asked 'Are you looking for your arm?' recognised that I had perceptual problems. What she did not know was that I was unaware of my loss of body-image, and that I was dependent on other people to give me this information, as many times as I needed it, until I could comprehend my loss. If I had known of the deficit it would have helped. Perhaps I would not have understood immediately, but I think it would have been worthwhile.

I was aware that my doctor was testing me for 'sensory inattention' on the left side of my body. When he had finished I thought, 'I answered all those questions correctly'. This was because I felt whole and did not know that my brain had stopped processing information from my left side. I was not told of the areas where no response was registered by me.

A person is much more than a physical being. There are other aspects of ourselves that make us whole. Yet, in most hospitals and rehabilitation units, the physical aspect is given undivided attention by staff concerned with stroke rehabilitation. I consider this to be a gross oversimplification of the problem.

I believe that changes in the physical body take place when there are corresponding changes in awareness and attitudes. The patient with perceptual disturbances requires information so that an alteration in his self image will eventually come about. And with a new sense of being, feeling, thinking and believing, a new mental structure emerges.

When I yawned I had a reflex action. My left arm would slide across my stomach. I thought it was a snake. Because I did not realise my left side was there, I didn't look to the left. I wouldn't have thought the arm was mine even if I had looked. The silly part is, I'm really frightened of snakes but I wasn't frightened and didn't even wonder what a snake was doing in bed with me. Most of the time I just seemed to be witnessing what was happening and did not have the energy to become involved. Perhaps the confusion seemed too great to surmount.

It was sheer hell for me, and the nursing staff too, when the lights were turned off at night. I was continually summoning them with the buzzer. I thought I was going to fall out of bed and I was in pain. I was continually being told: 'It is only a few minutes since you last called me'. Nobody realised the problems confronting a person with loss of body-image. I was unaware of the left side of the bed or the left side of myself, feeling I was lying on a narrow plank. It's terrible to be trapped in terror and unable to show any outward signs. The nurse didn't understand—to her everything appeared all right—and I was making a fuss without good reason. Had she understood the problem she may have been able to help me grasp the concept—but my mind was not recognising or accepting the existence of the whole of the hospital bed or my body on it. My problems could have been minimised by the provision of a night light. I could not correct my position into a balanced, supported one. How different it might have been if we had all been aware of my loss of body-image.

Since I responded to touch on my left side, I can't help but think that if pillows had been placed down the left side of my body, touching my skin, they may have been the cue I needed to make me feel secure. The pillows would have informed me of the true boundary of my body.

In the first week, as I recall, my days were spent slumped in a wheelchair or flat on my back on a trolley, being transported to different units in the hospital for tests to determine the cause of my stroke.

Nuclear medicine and brain scans were frightening terms to me, and I don't remember anyone explaining what the procedures would involve. Perhaps they may have thought I would not understand. But it was my right as a living human being to be told exactly what these terms meant.

The brain scan was a long and terrifying experience. I felt tired and very insecure and fearful when being wheeled, at what seemed to me a fast pace, down corridors and into lifts. The corridors seemed miles long. Then, the brain scan. The scanner, which was round and about 80 cm across, was lowered to within about 3 cm of my face. I was afraid of falling off the narrow metal table. I needed to see my body to feel secure and whole but was not aware that it was my loss of body-image which made me insecure. Later, I felt particularly helpless and heavy when the X-ray technicians were endeavouring to place me in the proper position for neck X-rays. Still later, it was the spinal tap which finally revealed that my stroke had been caused by a cerebral haemorrhage.

I find it incredible that staff—doctors and nurses—are not aware that you listen intently to all they say to each other. That you wonder about the things they plan to do to you. You recognise that you are vulnerable—trapped and at their mercy.

I lay face down on the hospital bed, having been made ready by nurses for a spinal tap. A doctor and nursing sister approached my bed. I couldn't see them, but I heard their voices. I knew she was a sister because he addressed her in this way. She sat on the bed beside me, held my hand and told me not to be afraid. Neither one introduced themself to me. I only heard their voices. The sister said, 'Where is Doctor X? He usually does this'. The doctor replied, 'He's away for a few days and to tell you the truth I haven't done one of these for ages. I've almost forgotten how'. After a few minutes and a good deal of muttering on his part, he said 'I think that's the spot, now with a little help from Him up there we'll go in and see what we get'. I also prayed that it was the right spot.

They are both still faceless people to me. The only words the doctor addressed to me were, 'Nurse will turn you onto your back in a few minutes, Mrs Hewson. You will remain on your back for a number of hours. Try not to move, it could be dangerous. You could also get a very bad headache'.

Did they think I was no longer a feeling, thinking human being?

It is only now, nine years later, that I can write about this. Before, I was still caught in the emotion of this experience. I couldn't bear to write of it because of terror trapped in my mind.

I still had skin sensation. If someone touched me on the left side I felt it, but couldn't locate the spot they touched unless I looked. Of course I didn't look to the left unless I was told to; to me it wasn't there. It was most uncomfortable to look to the left, and I felt under stress and agitated when I did. I needed recognition of my problems by the staff and also their assistance in giving me an understanding of these problems.

The highlight of my day was when my husband Ray was beside me. He came before work in the morning in time to give me my breakfast. After his working day was over he came to help me with my evening meal. He would then sit beside me and stroke or massage my left arm with his tender, sensitive hands.

Quite often while he was doing this I would lapse into sleep, only to waken when he removed his hands from my arm.

Neither Ray nor I realised that in stroking my arm he was making me aware of the space my whole body occupied and reinforcing the message that my left arm was really there. When I no longer received this message through his fingers, I would awake and feel distressed and insecure. Communication through touch on my affected side gave me security.

How do you tell someone about loss of body-image when they are ill and in pain, with little concentration? Massage and stroking became the first communication of this to me. Through someone else's fingers I was becoming aware of the left side of my body. Had this massage and stroking been constantly reinforced with a verbal commentary of which part of me was being touched, and had I been encouraged to look and see, I think it would have paid dividends. Touch is very important.

My bed was beside a window which was on my left. I didn't look that way, but I do remember hearing the waves breaking on the beach below. I always asked for the window to be left open a little and would get Ray to check this before he left. I needed to feel the breeze on my face. Perhaps the softness of the gentle breeze touching my face and arm gave me a sense of wholeness. I do know I became upset when the window was closed. The breeze felt like the touch of God. It was my only contact with nature. I had always loved the sea and the sand, the sky and the wind. I often wondered if the breeze coming through the few centimetres of open window would be the closest I would ever be to these lovely things again. It was winter, and with the window open, everyone else in the ward shivered to allow me my breath of life.

At night when the visitors had gone, the three other people in my ward would receive a sleeping tablet. I was informed by the sister that my doctor didn't believe in them. There could well have been a valid reason for this statement, but I was not told. I needed a really solid explanation to justify my unrelieved suffering and tremendous pain. If drugs and medications were injurious to me, some alternative methods to induce sleep should have been tried. Perhaps the use of sedative drugs might have added to my problem of muscle weakness. But if these alleviating drugs were denied to me, then psychological help should have been given to allow me to sleep.

On looking back, I now believe a great proportion of my pain was caused by wry neck. For the first few days I lay with my head fallen to one side. I was unable to alter this position myself. At one time I was put in a neck-support collar, but it was far too large and I would disappear into it, up to my eyes, feeling starved for air. No smaller collar was available. My husband needed to use both hands to lift and move my head. It felt so heavy and I was so helpless. The X-rays had shown disc degeneration in my cervical spine, and with my head in this static, unnatural position, I think the condition known as wry neck resulted, causing extreme pain. From the very first moment of hospitalization I needed correct positioning to reduce physical complications and additional severe pain. I believe that tension trapped in my body because of unexpressed emotion was also a contributing factor to the pain I felt. The inclusion of a psychologist to a Stroke Rehabilitation team would be beneficial to patient, family and staff.

I believe that rehabilitation should begin immediately after the first moment of stroke. Certainly physiotherapy, occupational therapy and nursing are the keystones of rehabilitation.

Until the cause of my stroke had been diagnosed, I had been receiving limited physiotherapy and occupational therapy in the ward. I can well remember the relief provided by the warm packs placed 'somewhere'. I also had some respite from pain when placed in what I now know to have been a semi-prone position with the infra-red lamp on the back of me 'somewhere'. I presume it was placed somewhere behind me. Locations behind me were jumbled and unreal.

So that I could make progress, it was necessary to find a starting point. I was unable to carry out any given task. The level of difficulty was too high for me. You can't take someone from kindergarten and place him in high school and expect good results. A nurse said to me one evening, 'Lorna, I hope you are

doing some deep breathing. Every cell in your body needs oxygen . . . and, oh boy, do your cells need oxygen'. She not only suggested something I could do, but she also gave me a good reason for doing it. My first success was in taking a deep breath. When I succeeded in carrying out an instruction, it was the starting point. One of the basic principles of retraining is finding the level of the patient's capabilities and starting from there. Now I was on the long, long road back.

Again it was a nurse who reminded me of the value of meditation. Prayer and meditation were very valuable to me, not only for the spiritual benefits received, but because they gave me a focal point other than self, discomfort and pain. This escape was only of short duration, but even a brief remission was a positive help.

I think that learning to relax my body and mind by using special relaxation techniques would have helped me enormously before my stroke, perhaps even averted it. During my second week I was taken daily to the Physiotherapy and Occupational Therapy Departments for retraining. I received their expert services for five days each week. I felt like a heavy blob and was unable to carry out instructions given me. My concentration span was short; pain and tiredness constantly overwhelmed me. Being unaware of my loss of body-image and the problems that it incurred meant delayed rehabilitation. I am sure I made small gains in these first two weeks, although at the time I felt there were none. Without the help and knowledge of the health professionals who cared for me, I could not have made much progress. Without love and friendship from my husband, family and friends, I'd have had little reason for living. My motivation sprang from their love, their calm and positive attitude, their belief that all would be well. I was still dear to them. No matter what the outcome, we would manage.

I believe, however, there is much additional knowledge concerning loss of body-image to be discovered, and I hope that in some measure I may be able to help in this. Other hemiplegics may derive much insight into their condition through these investigations and discoveries.

Would I ever read again? I asked Ray to bring me the evening newspaper each night. I had difficulty in holding it in one hand, so he would separate the pages and fold them in half. I would just stare at a page and then turn to the next. I was not reading a thing. I went through all the motions but nothing happened. I wondered why, but was unable to untangle the problem. Ray realised that my eyes were not moving. I could not scan.

When I first started to read again, my eyes would move only about half-way along a line, and then perhaps jump several lines. About five weeks after my stroke, I began to read simple, short articles; they started to make some sense. By the ninth week, I was reading parts of books. In the tenth and last week of my stay in hospital, I read a complete book, *The Moon's a Balloon*.

During the first four weeks I was both inundated and preoccupied with pain. At the same time I appeared outwardly unemotional. I shed no tears. I smiled no smiles. I tried to

> Dear Lorna   29·11·83
>
> I wish to thank you most sincerely for the trouble you have gone to on my behalf. I am enclosing a couple of clean tapes tapes tapes as replacement the G tape is not worth best but they are the cheapest at this point of time. I have followed your advice to listen to the tape daily very beneficial in from strength & sleep I am yours sincerely

understand and carry out the retraining techniques. I tried so desperately that these efforts absolutely exhausted me. I remember my doctor saying to me, 'You get an "A" for trying'.

A critical part of rehabilitation surely must be the communication and teamwork between the doctor and health professionals and the patient. In addition to this there must be a special human relationship between patient and doctor. The patient should have a definite right to privacy with the doctor so that personal questions may be answered and worries resolved. The patient *must* have the opportunity to speak with the doctor alone, and to be recognised as a human being, with the absolute right to be treated as such. Only by being acknowledged as a complete person can the patient move into the process of rehabilitation. Naturally, it is necessary for the doctor to discuss the patient's situation with the trained staff. Often, however, during the doctor's rounds, the patient finds that the doctor has moved on to the next bed before he (the patient) has even put into words some question of great concern.

In the acute stage of stroke, there is need for:
* Recognition by staff of individual problems
* Pain relief
* Correct positioning to prevent dysfunction and complications
* Information—communicated by methods which are positive and purposeful.
* Touch communication on the affected side to build security
* Breathing techniques, because every cell in the body cries out for oxygen
* Relaxation, for it is through this practice that both mind and tight muscles are relaxed
* Meditation, or quietness of mind, to gain insight.
* A realisation by all—stroke family and professional staff—that man is more than a physical being; there are other aspects of being human, they must be acknowledged and addressed, given equal attention during stroke rehabilitation. There must be interaction between the physical, mental, emotional and spiritual or intuitive aspects of ourselves. Then integration results, we are fuctioning as a whole.

Horror trip between two hospitals

Quite often we choose to stay at a place or with certain people because we are familiar with their ways and know the layout of the establishment. Even if you feel 'not understood' it is tempting to stay put.

I was uneasy at the prospect of being transferred to another unit some distance in kilometres from the hospital I had been in for four weeks.

Part of my uneasiness stemmed from encouragement by therapists, some of them friends, to stay. My doctor and the nursing staff encouraged me to go. Both had valid reasons, all were looking at what would be best for me, all believed in their own system. They were all insensitive to the way this affected me.

At the slightest suggestion that this move was imminent I begged to stay just a little longer. In fact I was granted a reprieve of twenty-four hours—then the ambulance arrived to carry me off—my friends shook their heads; I imagined them saying 'What a pity'. The hospital (Rehabilitation Unit) were alerted of my impending arrival.

A nice young ambulance man wheeled a stretcher to the side of the hospital bed, and by his side was a ward sister. She instructed him to put my clothing, radio, television set and books on the stretcher and said I should sit in the front of the ambulance beside him.

Seated in the front beside the driver, my possessions riding on the stretcher in the body of the ambulance, we pulled away from the curb—the nightmare trip began.

It became increasingly apparent that advice given by the sister was wrong. I had no sitting balance. Every swerve or curve to the right or left unbalanced me. I flopped against the driver or crashed onto the door on my affected side. Either way I was unable to regain a stable sitting position. Most distressing and uncomfortable for me and for the ambulance driver. Many times he pulled in to the curb to adjust my body position. He made haste in as gentle a manner as possible. On reaching our destination we were both exhausted. Without doubt he informed the admitting sister in graphic detail of our journey between hospitals.

A wheelchair was brought to the side of the ambulance. I remember the sister's kindness—very soon I was tucked up in bed.

Later I was to learn that my reputation had gone before me. 'Wait until you get her!' I was classed as a difficult patient; I couldn't sit up straight in a chair or maintain a balanced position in the hospital bed—I was frightened of falling out of bed and continuously complained of pain that I could not locate in my body.

Quite often the patient is labelled as 'bad' because hospital staff don't understand the problem.

We don't use wheelchairs here...

This part of my story is about my survival and progress in a rehabilitation hospital. I think of this rehabilitation unit with a great deal of affection, because it was there I started on my real road to recovery.

On the afternoon of my arrival at the rehabilitation hospital the doctor on duty not only gave me a thorough medical examination, but she also prescribed for me a simple medication—Valium—which relieved the pain in my tortured muscles by relaxing them. From the moment of stroke, my muscles had been racked by cramp and spasm. No effective pain-killing medication had been given for this, despite repeated requests from me and my family. My new doctor had the courage to prescribe a very small dose of Valium (only 2mg, three times a day, later reduced to 2mg a night), but it was enough to ease the excruciating pain which had until then remained with me continually. Without pain, I had hope and a chance to comprehend the instructions that I had to follow in order to recover.

In this initial interview my new doctor asked me questions designed to assess the degree of confusion in a patient's mind. I had been waiting for these questions, which I knew so well from my experience in the role of questioner when I myself was working as a member of the Occupational Therapy Department. It was strange what an extraordinary importance I now placed on answering these questions satisfactorily.

Some questions asked were, 'Do you know what hospital you are in?' 'Can you tell me today's date?' 'Do you remember the name of the Prime Minister?' There were a number of general questions like this. Each day when my husband arrived at the hospital my first question, and sometimes my only one, would be, 'What is today's date?' I felt that it was important for me to answer these questions correctly to prove that I was not stupid, because I felt like a dunce. It was my loss of body-image and lack of awareness of my left side that made me feel this way.

I found the change to an unfamiliar environment and staff a little alarming. I was now in a large ward of about twenty beds, filled with people stricken with varying degrees of disablement. That first night I remember was very noisy. There were no buzzers attached to the beds, and there always seemed to be someone calling for a nurse. To me it was like Bedlam. Nurses soothed demented patients by singing them nursery rhymes. I was soon to discover that this rehabilitation unit was a very public place.

With pain gradually diminishing thanks to the medication prescribed, I started to sleep a little at night and life became more bearable. The night staff at this rehabilitation hospital were absolutely fantastic. I think the difference may have been that in this hospital the nurses worked the night shift by their own choice. In the General Hospital the nurses worked on a less flexible roster system. They seemed resentful when on night duty, perhaps because they were missing the pleasures they normally shared with their family and friends. Also, the General Hospital night shift seemed to be understaffed, and those on duty did not like being asked to do work they considered the day staff should have done.

In the acute stage of my illness in the General Hospital, one nurse and one sister had intimidated me. They were bearable when not on duty at the same time, but when they worked together it was intolerable. They were the only staff I remember who 'put me down'. One night this particular nurse removed the ear plug of my radio from my ear and then put the radio out of my reach, saying, 'It's time you went to sleep'. I had found a way of coping with my inability to sleep due to pain: it was with the diversion of my radio. I could well have been spared the removal of this small aid which I used to keep my sanity when all my independence had gone. What a difference there was in the quality and kindness of the night staff in the Rehabilitation Unit. They were superb.

Rehabilitation was taking place twenty-four hours a day, with emphasis on everyday activities which would confront us on our return home. Most of the staff were experts in rehabilitation. The basic retraining system was simple and workable and one in which I was able to make progress. There was a much greater degree of team work here between the occupational therapy and nursing staffs than in the General Hospital. The Physiotherapy Department worked with a different approach and method, and I derived great benefit from the techniques that were used. I could not, however, have progressed far with my rehabilitation without the help of all of these teams.

The occupational therapy staff, with the cooperation of the sisters and nurses' aides, concentrated mainly on teaching me to use the resources which remained on my unaffected right side. This form of rehabilitation had been developed over a number of years by a highly skilled occupational therapist, a lady with great insight into the needs of the disabled person. She knew how important it was for the patient who had become disabled to feel secure when learning the techniques of transferring from bed to chair, and how to go about taking the first faltering steps. Diversional therapy (recreation and handcrafts) was also under the guidance of the occupational therapy staff.

Methods used by the physiotherapist to stimulate the left side of my body were many and varied. I benefited because this was the side that I did not know about and it was essential for me to learn of its existence. I was totally unaware of it as part of me and I did not realise that I was unaware. Ice packs bandaged to my foot and left leg didn't have much meaning. I didn't shiver then, but I do now when I think of it. The physiotherapist would stroke my left hand and slap it and tap it. I enjoyed what she was doing, but I didn't understand the reason for my pleasure, which was that the physiotherapist was showing me the position of my arm and leg in space. As soon as she stopped touching me I felt uncomfortable and distressed. I didn't know why. I can remember doing range-of-movement exercises with my left arm supported in a sling which was attached by a spring to an overhead bar. My physiotherapist seemed to treat me as a whole person, and I felt more myself when I was with her. However, what I still needed was someone to explain to me what loss of body-image was all about.

When the health professionals are considering a rehabilitation program for patients who have loss of body-image, independence of movement is certainly extremely important (i.e. transferring from bed to chair, transferring body weight, walking, etc.). What concerns me is re-establishing in the patient's mind that the whole body is there. The longer the mind is denied this knowledge, the more difficult it becomes for the patient to progress. In my opinion, muscular movement without consciousness of what is moving brings few lasting results. I think it is highly important that the key staff in a rehabilitation unit do not become insensitive to the needs of each individual, and do not insist on the patient conforming to an already established pattern which may not actually meet individual needs. Each person admitted as a patient is unique and should be treated as such. And I believe that changes in ideas and concept should be taking place constantly within the framework of the highly skilled team. Communication must be good between all rehabilitation services and they should have respect for each other's methods and treatment. This leads to a secure, relaxed atmosphere in which the patient can progress.

My first morning in the rehabilitation unit stands out in my memory. The sister who came to my bedside said, 'We don't use wheelchairs here unless absolutely necessary. You are going to walk to the breakfast table'. She was positive in her approach and definite in her instructions. She gave me confidence. I walked with the aid of my four-legged friend, a wooden pylon, and the sister directed my every move.

What an aware person she was! At a glance she saw my weak areas. To enable me to put one foot in front of the other and walk, she would lock my left knee with her hand to stabilise my leg, thus allowing me to stand on it. Then she would bring my right leg forward. I could not locate my left leg because it was behind me and I couldn't see it, hence didn't know it was there. So she would move it for me. It was in this manner that we progressed to the breakfast table. I was tired but realised that with the help and expertise of this sister I had achieved in one morning more than I had in the previous four weeks. My ability to move was, and is, important to my own self-esteem. It took me a long time to learn to bring my left hip and leg forward so that I could take a step.

After breakfast I was taken in a wheelchair to have my shower. In this unit, half of the patients showered before breakfast, the other half afterwards. I regarded the nurses who showered us as beings from outer space. They wore large rubber aprons and black knee-high rubber boots. I was soon to learn why they were decked out in this attire. It afforded some protection from patients like myself who, when they were given a handheld shower, splashed water on everything and everybody except themselves. My first lesson in showering myself and not the nurse took place that morning, and, although I was physically exhausted afterwards, mentally I was exhilarated. I was learning to care for myself, and each morning I was encouraged to do more for myself. Thanks to this method of rehabilitation I could make small advances every day in the essentials of everyday living.

Strange to say, it was these same nurses who seemed to have a lapse of memory whenever they had deposited me on a lavatory. They would disappear, sometimes never to return. Their stock phrase was always, 'I'll be back in a minute'. I threatened to expose the lot of them and write a book called *Death on a Toilet Seat!*

After my shower I was wheeled to the recreation room. The staff who worked in this area were occupational therapy aides and nurses. They all liaised with the Rehabilitation Sister. It was a good team. When I was admitted, the occupational therapist who had helped establish the retraining method used in this unit was on long-service leave. With great kindness she returned once or twice a week to help with my rehabilitation.

She must have left the hospital many times wondering if I would ever learn. She would return in a few days to find I was able to follow through the movement which I had been unable to accomplish before.

I needed a lot of time to understand and plan what was then, to me, a complicated manoeuvre. I was embarrassed because I was unable to carry out simple instructions. I used to sit and think, 'If only they would instruct me in a different way, or use different words, I might understand. Somehow I must be able to rearrange my brain to do this'. Part of my difficulty was that I was still unaware of my loss of body-image. Still no one tried to explain that to me. I now realise it was because there is so very little known about this aspect of stroke.

I hope that through my experience others may not have to undergo the terrible period of being unaware that their perception of their body has altered. They should be brought to an awareness of the meaning of loss of body-image as soon as possible.

My concentration span was still short, and I found it easier to carry out instructions if they were given in simple terms by someone standing on my right. Even then it was important that they allowed me considerable time and quietness in which to concentrate on the movement required. Without pain I could think in a more positive and constructive manner. I needed to think of each move I made. I needed to think the movement through and then endeavour to carry it out. Sometimes it took me days of rehearsal until I could carry out an instruction. I learnt by repetition, but a new ability appeared when I became aware of what I was doing.

Our mornings were spent alternating between handcraft and retraining. It was a good system, and all the activities took place in one large room. Down each side of the room long tables were placed: the gentlemen were seated on one side of the room, the ladies on the other. God alone knows why we were segregated. Perhaps they feared we might become 'sexophrenics'! It was at these tables that the occupational therapy aides would instruct and assist us with the craft of our choice or, in some cases, the craft chosen for us. If the product did not come up to their standard, they would secretly whisk it away and correct the work we had so laboriously attempted. The work would then be returned to us, looking perfect, but it was not our own effort. Some years before, I had done much the same when I myself had been an occupational therapy aide in this same Rehabilitation Unit, but it was soon brought home to me, with considerable mental anguish, the effect this was having on the patients.

The first morning that I myself was a patient in that same recreation room, it was suggested by a member of staff that I do some cane weaving, and I agreed to make a basket for my grand-daughter. That morning I managed with difficulty to produce two rows of weaving. I was so slow; the cane dried out and the weaving was loose. I thought to myself, 'That's all right. I'll use it as a gauge to judge my own progress'. The next day, when the basket was placed in front of me, I had nowhere to progress. It had been made perfect by a very well-meaning staff member. Actually, by this action she was implying that I would not notice the difference. It made me feel that others also thought my intellect had been badly damaged because I had suffered a stroke. Once more I cried out inside, wondering why they regarded me in this way.

I found the exercises I did at the push-up bar most beneficial when given with the guidance of an expert. To enable me to walk, a back-slab was bandaged to my left leg to lock my left knee back. Then, with the nurse on my left side, the sister on my right, and my pylon in my right hand, we would make our way across the recreation room to the push-up bar. What a trio we made! I was glad when we arrived at the bar and eager to sit down and rest awhile. For a period of time, that first walk of the day was done with the support of the back-slab. It would then be removed and not used again that day.

A lot of my retraining was to be done at the push-up bar. With the help of the nurse, I would rise from the chair and try to capture an upright position. One exercise was rocking from side to side. This was to teach me how to transfer weight from one leg to the other. I could not do any of these movements without the help of a nurse, and, in the beginning, two nurses. When I moved my weight over to the left side of my body, it was frightening. I felt like an amputee without a left leg to stand on. I would think, 'God, where's my leg? I haven't got one'. Then the nurse would tell me to put weight through my left leg—which didn't seem to be there. Is it any wonder I felt stupid and bewildered?

It was not until about two and a half years after my stroke that I was able to feel my weight going through from my left hip to my left heel. Even now to feel weight going through I must have both feet on the ground and the weight of my body evenly distributed. If I lean to my strong right side, I feel like an amputee. I must stand erect to feel whole.

Centre of gravity shift was a problem of great magnitude. The more weight I put on my unaffected right leg and the more I leaned into the right side of the world around me, the less chance I had of correcting the gravity shift and returning to my true centre of equilibrium. Re-establishing balance is dependent on correct body knowledge being communicated to the brain. Then you can sit straight in a chair and walk with your body in an upright position. A wonderful feeling of security occurs. Once more you can stand without fear of toppling over! The energy and concentration required to stand and walk erect can be diverted to more enjoyable pastimes.

Kneeling, distributing weight evenly through all four limbs, has helped me regain a sense of 'knowing' my body.

At the time of my stroke, during the ten weeks I was hospitalized as well as the two years I was an out-patient, physiotherapists and occupational therapists encouraged me to try and adopt this position. Apart from the fact that I could not move my leg without seeing it, my left shoulder and elbow were unstable, so also were my left hip and knee. Two years after my stroke the prospect of achieving stability in the crawling position was remote.

When I commenced Yoga and for some years afterwards I

avoided adopting positions that were dependent on me being on 'all fours', knowing I couldn't do this. In 1982, six years after my stroke, I tried again. My God, I could do it.

Regular massage by Ray kept muscles in reasonable condition, stimulated nerve endings and improved circulation in my left arm, leg and buttock. The Yoga programme I carried out each morning strengthened other parts of my body and helped me rebuild an awareness of muscle movement—contraction and extension. I became aware of the mechanics of movement, not just movement itself.

I believe the whole body is healing, recovering and re-discovering itself. This may be slow and go unnoticed but the outcome at some time in the future could be that you can do something you couldn't do before.

Just keep trying!

At 11.30 a.m. every available nurse arrived in the recreation room. Our meal time was approaching and their objective was to move us from the recreation room to the dining room. Those of us who were able to walk without the assistance of a nurse were encouraged to do so. Some of us walked only half-way and then wheeled the remainder in a wheelchair. What a little band of hope we were! All moving at our own pace and in our own peculiar fashion. All leaning in different directions as we walked with our own individual gait. People who were unable to walk at all were whizzed past us in their wheelchairs.

Our dining room was long and narrow. It had once been a veranda. It was hot and airless and left a lot to be desired. A rest period of about an hour and a quarter followed our mid-day meal. I am sure this was appreciated by all. It certainly was by me. The activities in the recreation room started again at 2 p.m. The group exercise class was conducted too quickly for me. I could not keep up with them. I would still be trying to get my thumb and forefinger to meet by the time most people had been through the whole range of excercises with both hands. There were quite a few patients like myself who just could not keep up. I think the program could have been given in two segments:

the slow ones in one group; and the slow, slow ones in another. It was just as important for me to get my two fingers to meet as it was for somebody else to complete the whole range of exercises.

After exercises came the part of the day I personally objected to, but which the majority of the patients loved: housie, beatles or dominoes. This is where the pre-stroke personality must be considered. I had never relished any of these activities. As a matter of fact, I avoided them like the plague. My leisure time had always been spent outdoors or with my head in a book, and to be wheeled to a table to play housie and to be told, when I begged to be excused from this form of torture, 'This is the group activity for the day, and you must conform', was a most frustrating and infuriating experience. I was unable to walk away from it. I was immobile and this made me angry. The anger which was within me acted as a great motivational force; it was the first emotion which I felt and expressed. I realise that a certain amount of system is necessary in a rehabilitation hospital, but this regimentation and lack of flexibility nearly drove me mad.

Fortunately, with the cooperation of the physiotherapist, I was able to spend most afternoons in the Physiotherapy Department, and this, to me, was so very worthwhile. Later, I would be wheeled back to the recreation room by a hall porter and would invariably arrive just in time to have a little more walking practice. Then I would wait for the rehabilitation nurse and ask her to walk with me on the way back to the ward. Most days she would do this. I found the instructions she gave me at this time were invaluable. There were only the two of us. All the rush and bustle of the day was over. She gave her instructions simply and clearly; because there was no noise, I could follow them more easily. She would lock my left knee back and then say, 'Lorna, your left leg is strong; trust it'. It was almost a command. She gave it; I obeyed. It was five weeks before I was able to walk the entire distance between the recreation room and the dining room. When I accomplished this, I felt a great sense of achievement.

At 4.30 p.m. we were seated at our tables for the evening meal. It horrified me that a bathroom which included lavatories was situated at the end of the enclosed veranda which served as our dining room. I felt ill at the sight of flies crawling all over tables, already set for our meal. To my horror, I saw people being forced to eat like animals because of lack of awareness on the part of some members of the staff. If a patient is unable to cut food into manageable pieces, then the staff should do this. Where possible, the patient should be taught to use a rocker knife which makes it easier to cut food into small portions. A non-slip mat should be placed under each plate to stop it from moving around in circles or skidding all over the table. Hygienically wrapped food is very difficult for a disabled patient to manage, but where there are no fly screens on doors or windows there is no other alternative. Since the initial publication of this book a change has taken place.

The disabled patient is even more disadvantaged by the obsolete structure of this building. The bricks that lined one wall were dirty, and the lino on the floor needed to be ripped up and replaced. This rehabilitation unit has so much to offer, but the walls are tumbling down around it. There is certainly something radically wrong with a State hospital system which allows this very old and crumbly cottage to be used as a rehabilitation hospital. The staff is good; the method is good; the buildings are shocking.

Because of my disablement and fears, I would have preferred to see my doctor in privacy. I found it hard to demonstrate my walking ability when my doctor asked me to do so. This was because there were always six or seven other health professionals with him. It was difficult to concentrate on walking in front of so many onlookers, particularly if they were talking among themselves. My concentration span was short, and I needed calm and quietness in which to demonstrate my meagre, hard-earned skills. I had to think each movement through and needed time to do so. I was much happier if my doctor directed his questions to me rather than the sister. It was important to me to feel that he did not consider me intellectually disabled as well as physically disabled. When he came on his rounds, I seemed to be almost speechless. There were so many others there. I felt I was being put on show. The only question I remember asking him was, 'When can I go home?'

Returning to the critical question of relief from pain—it was in the early acute stages of my stroke that I became alienated from my doctor. When I was in extreme and unremitting pain, the staff told me that my doctor did not believe in pain-relieving drugs.

At that point, why didn't he, or a member or his staff who knew his reasons, tell me why? All I am asking of any medical practitioner who might read this is: 'Please, explain to your patient your reasons for whatever type of treatment you are prescribing. Please treat your patient as a rational human being'. When you are in pain, time stands still, filling your world with constant agony; when you are not in pain, time passes quickly.

I had always enjoyed work and now the very essence of work was the effort to learn to walk again. I was impatient with those who could not transmit to me lucid information which would give me the confidence and the security I needed to walk. I wanted to go home and needed the assurance that I was making progress in this direction. I wanted to walk away from untenable situations and needed the ability to do so. I wanted quietness to relearn previous skills. I needed solitude to give vent to my emotions.

As I mentioned previously, anger was the first emotion I expressed following my stroke. It was also while I was in this rehabilitation unit that I cried for the first time. I cried because I was sad at what had happened to me. It was also here that I laughed for the first time. I was slowly learning how to show outward response to the emotion I was feeling. I laughed at a show that was on TV. I had never laughed at this show before and have never since; but when I heard myself laugh for the first time, I just had to keep on doing it. I laughed on and off for about half an hour. How unalive we are when we don't know how to express happiness or sadness. It is important that someone explains the grieving process to the patient and to the family, that it's all right to feel angry. Sadness also is a natural response, but unresolved it can lead to depression.

These changes occur within all relationships, not only among the family but in friendships.

The stroke person could also be doing the distancing and breaking of bonds through loss of self-esteem and a changed self-image.

Recovery from stroke is more than a physical experience. The other subtle processes of mending need to be addressed.

I hated being a hemiplegic. I wanted to be the me that I used to be. I became depressed and anxious. The time could not come quickly enough for me to return home. My need for solitude was recognised by the staff, and I was transferred from the large ward into a small room on my own. It was in the quietness of this small room that I learned to dress myself. I learned how to transfer from my bed to the commode and was able to do this without assistance before I left hospital. But, best of all, I had time alone with my husband. It is hard to talk with the one you love in a public place, such as a twenty-bed ward. You know you will display emotion and you don't want to do this in public. It was also good to have my friends to myself. My husband, family and friends held me together.

The day came when my doctor asked Ray how he felt about taking me out for the day. We were elated. We were to have a trial run. The day when I would be discharged from hospital must be coming closer. One of the hospital wheelchairs was coaxed into the back of our small car. I sat tensely in the front seat, hanging on like grim death. Fortunately, the car had bucket seats which helped me to stay upright most of the time. When we took a right hand corner, I could stabilise myself with my right hand and arm, but when we went around a left hand corner I fell against the door, not knowing how to recapture my upright position again. The sight of the traffic moving so quickly along the road also seemed to upset my equilibrium. I found it better to close my eyes. The high-pitched sound of a motor bike put me on edge. Sounds with a high pitch still worry me. This is probably because I am still hanging on to the memory of the sound that I associate with the cerebral haemorrhage that resulted in my having a stroke. Excessive noise in a rehabilitation unit is bad for both patients and staff. A sound-proof room should be provided for this type of rehabilitation.

My husband and I had a wonderful day with a very good friend whose home was only a few miles from the hospital. We had spent many happy hours in her home and I thought I knew it like the back of my hand. This day was the beginning of a new way of thinking. I realised that going to a place which had once been familiar to me did not automatically make me feel safe and secure there. I have never regained the old relaxed feeling of just moving without thought. It was in the home of my dear friend Chris that I realised I had to learn to look and see in a new way. I had to develop awareness of every movement, every step.

What I missed so much that day was the ability to give my friend a spontaneous greeting, a good old hug and kiss. It is hard to hug with one arm and half a body. I had been trying to recapture things as they were before, and this was no longer possible. However, the joy of being with our friends on this my first day out was indescribable. It was on this day that something inside me whispered, 'You will be able to manage and survive outside'.

When we arrived back at the hospital, the evening meal was just being served. I was tired and quite glad to be back in that protected environment. Our day-out had shown me what a lot I still had to learn.

By now I was getting quite good return of movement in the fingers of my left hand. However, I needed to see my left hand to be able to use it. It was strange. My hand seemed isolated, and yet I was not concerned that I had a hand which seemed divorced from its arm. I was keen to see how I could use this hand that was all on its own.

The following weekend my husband drove me to our own home. I spent the whole morning making some coleslaw for lunch. God only knows how anyone ate it, but they did. It was coarse and unattractive. We had achieved a lot that morning because we had devised a way for me to cut the cabbage. This was to be part of the structure of our lives from that time on. Ray was always creating ways to allow me to function in a more independent manner.

It was exactly ten weeks after my stroke that I was discharged from hospital. Rehabilitation through learning techniques ultimately made it possible for me to choose alternative ways of living my life. I believe there is only one place to learn techniques which will eventually lead to greater independence: that is in a rehabilitation hospital. There they can teach you every method they know, but it is only by using your own initiative and using what you have that you progress. Fear of failure must be put aside, for it is only in stepping out into new areas with positive thought and an aware mind that life becomes bearable again.

Home again

Must I always live my life caught between crisis and challenge? This was the question I asked myself just one week after my return home. I had spent ten weeks in hospital, and during that time there had been one beacon shining brightly—home. My strong urge to return home was the source of my motivation for recovery. In that first week at home I realised that although I had achieved my goal, nothing had changed. I was still a severely disabled person with great limitations. That yearned-for event of 'going home' had worked no miracle. Had there been a magic wand somewhere to make that miracle happen, I am sure my husband Ray would have walked to the ends of the earth for it; that is, if I had allowed him out of my sight long enough for him to do so. I felt so insecure when he was not around. My poor, dear man! I demanded so much of him when I was trying to re-establish myself at home. I had to find my way to independence, and I could not do so without his help. During my ten weeks in hospital I had kept saying, 'I will be much better when I get home'. Now, here was the moment of truth. I was home. Until I was prepared to accept the truth and reality of my situation, I could not progress. I could postpone it no longer. It was the plan I made that day which allowed me to see a better tomorrow.

If other people could not see my situation, I had to discover it for myself. I needed a launching pad, a take-off spot, to create the right atmosphere in which I could progress. This was a task of great magnitude. When I had been an able-bodied person, home had presented no problems to me. Now it was filled with problems. No sooner would Ray eliminate one obstacle than another would appear. This occurred because I ventured into fields which brought problems in every new area I entered.

It was on a Wednesday afternoon in early November 1976 that I returned home. Five days later Ray returned to his work. Those five days were filled with trial and error, but tempered with joy at being home again. My first night in our bed was a nightmare of insecurity. Once more I was afraid I would fall out of bed. It was dark, and when I moved I didn't know how far I had moved, or what part of me had moved. It had taken me many weeks to learn to change my position while in bed. For some time I had been able to do this without help. Now, in just one night, I felt I had lost my independence of movement in bed. I was shattered. We had to ask ourselves why. Our bed was an innerspring mattress mounted on a spring base. Although we had always felt it was quite firm, we now realised that it was much softer than the hospital bed—and much too springy for me. When I moved, it moved with me. Because of this, I was unable to use the techniques I had learned. I needed a firm bed that would not move when I did. The next morning Ray bought a piece of timber 2 metres long, 1 metre wide and 3 centimetres thick. He placed it underneath the top mattress. This made an enormous difference. Another problem had been solved.

For many months, Ray was to have disturbed sleep at night. Sometimes when I was lying on the right side, my left arm would fall down behind my back. I had no strength in my shoulder muscles to hold my arm in a normal position. The result of my arm being in this abnormal position was pain. I was also unable to find my arm because it was under the blanket and I could not see it. I was therefore unable to move it; added to this, I had no muscles in my left arm to move. With the light out at night I was unable to visualise where my body was in the bed. I could not untangle this problem for myself and would need to waken Ray and ask him to find my arm and move it into a more comfortable position. The pain would cease, but the fear would not go away. I would lie there, afraid to go back to sleep in case the same thing happened again. I wish we had realised sooner what loss of body-image meant, and how important it was for me to see the part of my body I needed to move. A simple bed lamp or night light would have solved that particular problem so rapidly.

On returning home from hospital after a disabling illness, the patient, as well as other members of the family, has many problems to overcome. Problems don't go away if they are ignored. The longer they are left unresolved, the more insecure and depressed the disabled person becomes. Our manner of problem solving was—and is—to look at the area in which I am having difficulty, and then look at me and the way in which I move in that area. The idea is to put the area and me together, then look at both of them with awareness. It is by using this method that we can see and then understand why I have a problem. We are half-way there when we are able to recognise why the problem exists. We are then able to invent new aids or discover alternative methods for me to use. We still use this method of problem solving. We find that by tackling a problem and working out a solution to each difficulty as it arises, I am able to make progress. This, in turn, leads to a more interesting life because of my increasing independence.

When I was discharged from hospital, it was on the condition that there would be someone living close by who would be prepared to care for me. My immediate family offered to do whatever they could to help. Our youngest son, Pete, and his wife, Shell, lived only a few doors away from us. They have two little boys and at the time of my stroke, Andrew was four years old and Tim only four months old. Our elder son, Lincoln, and his wife, Joan, lived some few miles away and had two young daugthers; Melinda was five years and Sal not quite two. I knew my family was distressed at what had happened to me, and I feel sure they must have wondered how we would all manage. At no time did they give me the feeling I was a nuisance, and they always lent us the support we needed.

I felt sad that I was unable to give my grandchildren a proper cuddle. I wanted so very much to take them on my knee, put my arms around them and hold them close to me, to give them the love that was bursting within me. I felt so inadequate because I couldn't. I didn't want to be a grandma who could only sit in a chair. Melinda sometimes talks to me of the things we used to do together 'before you got sick, Ma-Ma'. Sal looks at me with her big brown eyes, her head covered with masses of curly hair, and I wonder what is going on in her mind. Andrew has always looked after me and seems to have the ability to anticipate my needs. He is my helpmate, so unusually perceptive. Tim, who is our youngest grandchild, is very clever at mimicking my walk. When he was younger, he would have such fun running off with my walking stick and hiding it. My spirit was always renewed by the energy, love and excitement which the children generated in our home. I would be tired because littlies are so active; nevertheless, they gave me something that was missing when they weren't around. I also think that I relived the times I had enjoyed with our own children when they were young.

When Ray returned to work, it was our next-door neighbour, Grace, who was my companion and helper. She was tireless in her efforts to help. Ray's day started early, and there were so many things he needed to do for me. Ray would give me breakfast in bed and then put the breakfast things away so that I could get out of bed. I needed to put on my lace-up boots to walk to the bathroom. I couldn't walk without these boots and sometimes had to put them on in the middle of the night if I needed to go to the toilet. Without my boots and my pylon, I could not move one step. I also needed Ray to help me hook up my bra. Sometimes in the mornings, I would put my nightie back on and climb back into bed. This did not happen often, as I felt so secure if I was up and dressed before Ray left for work. He set off at 7.30 a.m. and did not return until 6 p.m. in the evening. I can't help but wonder how he managed. There was so much for him to do. I am blessed indeed to have such a mate. When I say this to him, he replies, 'Remember, *we* had a stroke'. He certainly took me for better or for worse.

At 9 a.m. each morning my next-door neighbour would come in to check up on me. If I slept in, she would help me to finish my dressing; then together we would make the bed. Then she would do any of the things Ray had not had time to do. We could never have managed without her help.

My long hair posed an enormous problem. Goodness knows why I didn't have my hair cut sooner, after my stroke. It fell below my waist, and I had been in the habit of wearing it in a chignon on top of my head. To put my hair up on top of my head, it was necessary to gather it all up, then wind it around and put in a hairpin to secure it; then continue to wind it around itself. This action was repeated until it was in one large coil. Half way through this procedure I would fly into a tantrum. I would become irritated and toss my head, throwing my hair back. People thought I was dissatisfied with the manner in which my hair was being done. They were upset and couldn't understand what they were doing to cause this reaction. After all, they were doing their best for me. I was distressed with my behaviour which I couldn't justify. I knew people thought me ungrateful.

Have you guessed what caused this pattern of behaviour? It was my loss of body-image. When my long hair was being twisted around my head, it would fall in front of my eyes, thus intruding into my field of vision. I needed to see all of me to feel secure.

Before leaving hospital I had mastered the art of dressing myself, but I had not realised that a nurse always laid out my clothes on the bed within my reach. That first morning at home I tried to take my clothes from the wardrobe and was upset because I was unable to do so. I could not remove my hand from my pylon and look up, because in doing so I lost sight of my body, and, hence, was unable to maintain my balance. I wept. The task at which I had become so proficient while in hospital I could no longer do without the help of another person. I wept because there were so many things I was unable to complete without help. Everyone wanted to help me, but I wanted to be independent. Ray and Grace between them helped me to complete jobs I started but was unable to finish. I was quite often irritable and rude.

My very good friend Chris was a constant source of enlightenment. Some six years earlier, in 1970, Chris, who had always been a very active and independent person, had her left leg amputated above the knee. Since then she had walked a road filled with obstacles of all kinds. She had walked it with courage and determination and believed that I could do the same. The belief in me which Chris and my family shared kept me going. Chris knew what it meant to fight her way back. She inspired me with her optimism. In the first few days after my return home, I made the discovery that I was unable to feed myself unless someone took the food out of the refrigerator or the cupboard for me. This realisation did terrible things to my ego. Chris came to my aid immediately; that day she gave Ray an office chair which moved on large castors. Seated on this chair I was able to propel myself by using my strong right foot; this enabled me to reach into a cupboard, remove the food, place it on my lap and thus convey it to the bench. No sooner had I realised my problem than it had been dealt with by a very aware friend. We discovered that I could cope more easily with my disability if problems were solved quickly. I was impatient. I wanted so much to be independent again. It was the support from all who cared for me that helped me to make rapid progress.

    I had never realised how long it takes a disabled person to rise from a chair and get to the telephone. The frustration is great when, having manoeuvred this hazardous course and stretched out your hand, you find the phone suddenly silent. You are left wondering who was on the other end of the line and what exciting news of the outside world they had to tell you. Unfortunately, the next time the telephone rings you are inclined to try and make haste, and it is then you are in danger of falling. We made a point of telephoning our friends and letting them know I was home again. We told them of the problem I had in not being able to reach the phone before it stopped ringing, and we made the following suggestion: 'Let the phone ring out and then phone again'. Now, if the phone stops ringing before I can reach it, I don't worry. I know it is not a friend; perhaps just somebody selling something. I know my friends will ring back almost immediately. Each day when the phone rang at noon, I knew who it would be. For nearly two years Ray phoned me every day in his lunch hour to check that all was well.

I can remember the first day I spent totally alone. Ray had gone to work and my only close neighbour had gone out for the day. We had an empty house on the other side of us, with grounds overgrown with lantana. Our house was set well back from the road, and we had always enjoyed the privacy this afforded us. Now I didn't like that privacy one bit. I felt isolated, and would have loved to have a busy footpath running beneath our window. I feared that people passing by on the roadway would not hear me if I needed to get help. I walk badly when fear or tension are trapped within me, and I always need to remedy this situation immediately. The first question I must ask myself is, 'What are you afraid of?' That day the answer was loud and clear: 'Fire!'

Heat-wave conditions had reached a dangerous peak and the lantana and long grass growing next door would have burnt like tinder. We had steps at both the back and front of our house, and in those early days I was unable to manage them alone. I was afraid of being trapped in the house, unable to get out. Fear was overwhelming me, and I realised I must do something about it.

I telephoned the local fire brigade and told them of my predicament. They assured me of immediate assistance in case of fire and guaranteed to get me out of the house should anything happen. That was just what I needed at that moment. Someone to listen to me and reduce my fear. It was only then that I could make my long-range plans. I rang the local council and asked that the owner of the property be notified of the condition of his grounds and of the fire hazard they presented. Many phone calls and letters later, the owner came out to inspect his property, and it was with the help of my husband that it was eventually cleared. It is important for me to do something about a problem just as soon as I am aware of it. In dealing with my fear and insecurities in this way, I am able to reduce tension.

An outpatient

During the first week of my homecoming I decided I was not going to opt out of living. I had been home only a few days when I started to miss the hospital routine I had complained so bitterly about, and I missed the rehabilitation training I had been receiving while there. Our family doctor had known me for over twenty years, and he realised my need for continuing therapy. He referred me back to the Occupational and Physiotherapy Departments of the General Hospital where I had worked before my stroke. This was the hospital where I had first been treated in the acute stage of my illness.

The 11th of November, 1976, was my birthday, and it was on that day that I walked once again into the Outpatients' Department. I was now a patient where formerly I had been a staff member. I walked with the aid of my pylon and with my husband close beside me. This was the building I had walked into each morning going to work. I had never noticed the steep ramp at the entrance to the buildng. Now it proved to be a decided hazard to me. The black-and-white terrazzo floor throughout the outpatients' building worried me. Whenever I was confronted by a patterned floor-covering, I had difficulty in walking. The pattern seemed to make the outline of the floor indefinite, and therefore did not appear to provide me with a solid foundation to walk on. Believe it or not, this terrazzo floor took away my confidence in walking throughout the two years I attended the hospital as an outpatient.

Entering the doors that first morning as a patient instead of a member of staff was a sad time indeed for me. I sat down on a seat beside the lift, and I cried and cried. The change that had taken place in me was unbelievable. The last time I had walked through those doors was on the morning of my stroke. Would I ever achieve the freedom I had previously enjoyed? The lifts ascended and descended many times before I was able to control my crying. Then I couldn't walk because the tears didn't allow me to see where to place my feet. I cried in a public place; I was unable to make my way to a corner to hide my sobbing.

I attended the Occupational Therapy Department for one year and the Physiotherapy Department for two years. The staff of these two departments helped me to become aware of my perceptual problems. From them I learned that I had lost the ability to know where the left side of my body was in space. I was not denying the presence of this side of my body. It simply was not sending messages to my brain to tell me that it existed and where it was in space. With growing insight and knowledge many things began to come together in my mind.

Relentlessly I bombarded members of these two departments with questions. I was like a dog that hadn't eaten for a long time and now had been thrown a bone with a little meat on it. Greedy for more information, I wanted insight into my problems so that I could try to work them out. Although I was better able to understand my stroke than many patients, because of my experience as a technical assistant in occupational therapy, yet I found it hard to frame my questions. I discovered that many of the questions I asked my therapist were not answered satisfactorily. This led me to believe that little was known, even by professionals, about loss of body-image in stroke patients. Other hemiplegics, I found, were also having similar difficulty in this regard.

For the first year after my stroke, I attended the Physiotherapy and Occupational Departments two days each week. It was a most valuable experience. The techniques I had already experienced were added to, and I could more readily understand them in the light of my newly acquired knowledge. I knew that I had loss of body-image. I couldn't fully understand it, but just the knowledge of my altered space perception gave me a point from which to make a start.

In that first year I was to receive tuition and treatment from four different physiotherapists. I think I must have worn them out with my ceaseless questioning and endless chatter about things I was trying to understand. They were exceptionally good people and contributed immeasurably to my rehabilitation. My fifth and final physiotherapist was the person who guided me and helped me to unravel the constant problems forever confronting me. I would tell her of every new gain I had made, no matter how small, and I would discuss my disappointment about some tasks I had been unable to carry out. We would talk about my successes and my failures. Then we would analyse everything I had done. It was in this way that we were able to assess what I was doing correctly and also to see where I had gone wrong.

Other questions we debated were: was my progress due to improved concentration, added confidence, improvement in muscle strength or better co-ordination? Was it due to the application of ice-packs or heat-packs to my cramped muscles, my exercise routine, or the progressive improvement brought about by the lessening oedema in my assaulted brain? My physiotherapist talked to me about my perceptual problems. I am so grateful that she shared her knowledge with me. It was at this stage that I started to research into myself and my altered space perception. I had learned a little, but I had so very much more to learn. The whole program offered by the Physiotherapy Department was of immense help to me.

After my first tearful return to the Occupational Therapy Department I determined that henceforth I would wear a smile even if my heart remained heavy. It was difficult to be a patient in a department where I previously played such an active role. The staff were all old friends and workmates, and many of the patients I saw there each day were people I had helped only a short three months before. Then I had been physically fit and engrossed in my work. My erstwhile patients were sympathetic and I loved them for it, but at the same time I hated to be the person requiring their sympathy. I began to understand how much easier it is to give sympathy than to accept it.

My occupational therapist taught me how to get down on to the floor, where I did my daily exercises. More importantly, I needed to learn how to get up from this position. I think there are very few disabled people who have not had a fall. If they are alone when they fall, it is essential that they use a correct, safe method to get up again. If I fall when I am in company, I find it less embarrasing when I can get to my feet without help. It took me three years after my stroke to become quite competent at doing this. I now no longer need to lean on anyone or anything. Although I have a peculiar way of achieving this, the important thing is that it works. I am now able to sit on the sand or the grass, and when going on a picnic there is now greater choice of location; we are no longer restricted by many of my previous limitations. Thus, my freedom of choice is gradually being enlarged.

The equipment in the Occupational Therapy Department is mainly the type that may be found around anyone's home. During therapy I moved bricks, threw sandbags and climbed stairs; I did finger exercises and then gymnastics at the pull-up bar.

It was in this department that I tried to sew for the first time since my stroke. It was an odd experience. When my fingers were covered with material, they didn't seem to be there at all.

My fingers still disappear from my mind when they are covered by the garment I am sewing, but I now know that my fingers are there, even though they don't tell me so. In this manner I manage to do small repairs and hems. I am still not able to move the fingers on my left hand if they are hidden from view.

My occupational therapist accompanied me on my first bus trip. We travelled only three stops, just enough to give me the experience of boarding a bus, sitting down and then alighting. Afterwards, we made our way to the coffee lounge in a large department store where I was glad to sit down. As we sipped our coffee we talked of the difficulties I had encountered on this short trip. We walked back to the hospital, and in doing so I discovered that walking along a crowded footpath was a completely different experience from the walking I had been doing in a protected environment. I then made the decision to accompany my husband each week when he did the shopping at the supermarket.

I remember vividly that Thursday night shopping experience. Many times I nearly said 'Not tonight, Raymond George!' but I didn't give in to the fear and feeling of imbalance induced by fast-moving food trolleys, pushed by people who seemed to be in such a great rush. Anything moving quickly upset me. Sometimes I didn't know which was moving, me or the other people. It took many months of perseverance before I started to feel secure when shopping in a supermarket. Now, three years later, I am able to put my walking stick in my trolley, select the goods from the shelves, push the trolley to the checkout, pay the account, restack the trolley and push it out to the car.

I am unable to drive the car. The main reason is that I am still unaware of anything on the left. I have to remember to look to the left, and I quite often forget. When seated in a room full of people, I am very likely to ignore completely those sitting on the left of me. This is not because I don't see them; it is simply that I don't look to that side unless I specifically think of it.

I am very glad I was referred back to the hospital as an outpatient. I feel that my mental depression would have lasted much longer, and my progress slowed down, had I not been able to participate in the continuing rehabilitation offered by the hospital. On the first day of my return to the hospital as an outpatient, a large full-length mirror was introduced into my retraining program. It was in this mirror that I really saw myself for the first time since having my stroke.

I didn't like what I saw. I had the most terrible list to the right. I had been unaware of this angle of lean until I saw myself in the mirror. I needed someone to help me move into a more natural and balanced position and to remind and encourage me to observe and determine which way to move my body. I needed the awareness of how much better it felt to have my weight evenly distributed. It was necessary to learn how to do this and to develop an awareness of the whole pattern of movement. In the early days of my rehabilitation I needed encouragement to lean to my strong right side, because of my lack of awareness of the left side of my body. I felt confused when asked to keep my knee locked back and then to try and put weight through my left leg. My left leg didn't seem to be there, and I couldn't understand what the staff was talking about until my attention was drawn to my own reflection—listing to the right—in the mirror.

I became aware that the weight I felt attached to was actually me: *the left side of me*. It was not weight 'somewhere out there'; it was part of me. This was a profound revelation to me.

My physiotherapist constantly drew attention to my reflection in the mirror. She encouraged me to look at every movement I was endeavouring to make. As a hemiplegic, with loss of body-image, I was enabled by the mirror to see myself and the space my whole body occupied. The mirror became a magic mirror. It showed me things I was completely unaware of until I looked into it. I could now see why I couldn't get up out of a chair easily. Looking into the mirror I could see my left foot was caught around the leg of the chair. The mirror showed me I was leaving my left hip behind me when I walked and, therefore, walking like a crab. This miracle mirror let me see myself as others saw me.

With the aid of a mirror I get dressed more easily and more quickly. When I stand in front of the mirror I am able to check that my pants are pulled up to my waist on my left side and not left half-way down my hip, that my jumper is pulled down and everything tucked in. I don't use the mirror just for reasons of vanity, but of necessity. When the mirror is removed, I can't remember the image I saw in it.

I consider it essential that nurses, therapists, and all who are concerned with the patient having perceptual problems understand what stroke does to a person's concept of herself in space: the consequent loss of body-image.

Having a working background in a hospital rehabilitation department helped me understand at least some of the problems in this type of stroke. I feel sure that patients are saying, 'Please, help me to know how to move from here to there. Help me to understand why I can't perform this particular movement. Tell me what the word "stroke" really means'.

If there is one activity which I am sure is not mechanical, it is awareness. To make continuing progress, I had to learn how to look and see what I was doing. I stopped waiting and wishing for my altered space perception to return to its former state. I started to use what resources I had, combined these with the new knowledge I had acquired, and then moved into a new and hard-to-describe area of perception. I was aware that my whole body was not telling me the things it had told me before, but when I relaxed completely and listened, with an inner ear, it gave me a lot of information, although in a totally different way from anything I had ever experienced previously. I had been trying to understand my perceptual problems in 'normal' ways. Suddenly, things changed. My consciousness moved into an area of knowing. It was then I had to ask myself, 'What is going on in me that is different from the reality I knew before?'

I still felt insecure when walking on terrazzo floors and patterned carpets with definite contrasts of colour in the design. I had to ask myself, 'Why?' From my viewpoint, the floor appeared to have no solidity. The pattern seemed to be at different levels, or holes seemed to form in it. Now it takes me only a second to become aware of this. I have learned, in this case, not to believe what my eyes tell me. My eyes play tricks when I am in half-light. Once more, just as twilight falls, I need to distinguish fact from fiction.

When walking downstairs, at the moment when my left leg is poised in space my mind tells me that I have no leg. However, my new sense of awareness allows me to continue with the movement. When my foot reaches the next step, I am able to feel the weight of my body through my left leg and foot. My mind then accepts the left side of my body as part of me. Walking on sand, with its shifting surface, helped me to trust myself and allowed me to adjust to other soft and unstable surfaces. I still panic when I find myself in an unknown situation. It seems to happen automatically. I have now learned to stand still, relax, and ask myself, 'Why?' Using this method, I am able to work out solutions to my difficulties in a more rational manner.

I used to bump into the left side of doorways as I tried to go through them. I had my pylon on my right side and would not leave enough space for the left side of my body. I did the same thing with people if they were on the left side of me. I would never leave enough room for them beside me, and, of course, we would get jammed in the doorway. Why did this happen, I wondered? It took me a long time to realise that it was due to my altered space-perception.

I think there are different ways of perceiving reality. Because of my sensory disturbance, I had to invent for myself different methods of perceiving my new realities. In my search for alternative methods, I sometimes had to turn aside from the commonsense way that had been so familiar to me.

   Anything which intrudes between my eyes and my feet gives me the feeling that I am an amputee. It is then indeed that I panic: I don't know how to move my foot unless I can see it. Amputees know how to do this, because their nerves are still sending messages. There are any number of things which can interrupt my field of vision: someone holding my left arm can do it. If I am carrying a handbag or basket in my left hand, it hides my left foot. Taking a big step with my right leg makes it difficult for me to bring my left foot forward. It is too far behind me and, being out of sight, is lost. At times like this I find myself, as it were, 'listening inwardly' to find out where my left leg is. If I can relax and let go of panic, I am able to 'home-in' on it, but I am only able to use this method of 'homing-in' when I am completely relaxed.

   Another observation I have made is that my well-endowed bosom hides my left foot, and therefore makes walking difficult. The view of my foot is better if my bosom is saggy rather than uplifted. This observation leads me to assume that ladies who have loss of body-image and have small breasts have a distinct advantage over their more amply proportioned counterparts. Anything which interrupts my vision increases the risk of falling. I have difficulty in walking when wearing a long skirt. The division that slacks provide gives me the visual clues I need to enable me to walk. I have also found benefit from wearing shoes which contrast in tone and colour to my slacks.

   When walking through fly ribbons, often used in doorways, I find they interfere with the view of my whole body by falling across my eyes. I had the same problem when I stood on the inside of a rotary clothes line. I became trapped in the middle, surrounded by clothes, not knowing how to get out. With my right hand on my pylon, I was unable to brush the clothes aside. I couldn't duck underneath the clothes. My balance wasn't good enough. When I tried to push my way headfirst through the clothes, my vision was completely disrupted. Since my forehead was not used to coming in contact with such things, there was no message sent to my brain. I needed to know if the clothes would move. I also needed to know what was on the other side of them. My forehead sent no message to my brain regarding these things, and I always panicked. I have now learned to stand still, relax, and think calmly about the whole situation. I tell myself: the clothes are soft; they will move with me. Then I reason that there must be somewhere for me to walk out, because I walked in. There are many situations which I need to think through in this manner.

My ability to concentrate began to improve substantially some two years after my stroke. Prior to that time, I was only able to concentrate on one thing at a time. In fact, during the writing of this book I have noticed a dramatic improvement in my concentration span.

Examples of limited concentration span:

a) When walking, I didn't talk; and I didn't like people talking to me. I needed to concentrate on finding my left leg and moving it forward.

b) I could not rule a straight line. I could hold the ruler on the paper, but when my gaze shifted to the pencil, my hand moved. My hand moved with my eyes. This was a great frustration. In the intervening months I taught myself to print. I needed to be able to rule straight lines as they were necessary to set up my work. I kept trying, because I realised that I had mastered past difficulties by not giving in.

c) I had a strange experience about three years after my stroke. While sitting on the front seat in my friend's new car and talking to her excitedly about her new purchase, I was also trying to buckle my seat belt. I wondered why I was having difficulty in doing this. To my horror I saw that I had been trying to buckle my own left hand into the buckle fitting. My arm had evidently fallen down between the seat and the car door, and because I was talking and not concentrating I picked my hand up from the place where I had expected the seat belt to be. I still do not understand why my right hand did not get the correct tactile message.

d) To butter a piece of bread, I need to remove the butter from the container. The usual practice is to hold the container and steady it with your left hand, thus stopping the container from sliding around. My left hand seems to receive the message to hold, but not *what* to hold. Therefore, my hand is likely to hold anything that is close by, be it the bench top, the handle of a saucepan or anything else. It is when I realise that the butter container is still moving that I look from my bread to the container to see what is causing the problem. Then I have to mentally tell my hand *what* to hold. This is a daily occurrence, but I have become used to this pattern and no longer feel stupid because of the altered way in which I must perform simple tasks.

When a person suffers a sudden and disabling illness which is little understood by the health professionals, a greater understanding must be developed so that we may venture along new pathways. To allow this to happen, a unity must develop between the patient and health professionals: doctor-patient; nurse-patient; therapist-patient. It is a case of letting someone else into your brain: a very personal and private experience which requires a great desire for understanding the human condition. I was fortunate to have this type of relationship develop and grow to produce greater insight into the phenomenon of stroke and subsequent loss of body-image.

The rehabilitation hospital where I spent six weeks, and where I received intensive retraining, is known throughout Australia for its unique methods of management. So much time was involved teaching other staff from all parts of Australia that a special Education Team was developed.

In mid-1977 the Education Team invited me to become associated with the program. I had talked to the members of this team about my search into myself which, of course, was only just beginning. I talked to them about my areas of need which had not been met by the health professionals, and they helped me probe into the different aspects of my stroke. I was continually investigating and trying to understand my difficulties, and I may have been quick to blame and slow to give praise to the staff who looked after me during my stay in hospital.

The Education Team listened to my story, and between us we began to understand a little more about the difficulties confronting me and others who suffered similar experience due to the phenomenon of non-dominant parietal lobe stroke.

The team recognised the value of patient participation, and many things which had puzzled both the team and myself started to unravel. The team gradually began to integrate this completely new concept into the education program.

A little surprise

I had now been home for about six months and although it took me a long time I received great pleasure in doing simple things.

I enjoyed demonstrating my newly acquired skills by making afternoon tea or pouring a cool drink for friends who called in for just a few moments. It was also a way to encourage them to stay a little longer. I missed the stimulation of being with people and hearing about ordinary events that were taking place in their lives, perhaps boring to them but stimulating to me.

Six months is a time that stands out in my mind. Friends called less often, people I had known for many years were gradually dropping out of my life. Some were saddened by what they thought of as my unrealistic expectations of recovery to a state where I could join them in going places and doing things. One such 'friend' said, in a marked querulous tone, 'Lorna, don't you think it's time to face facts and realise you will not improve very much more? Stroke is like that. I have nursed many people with strokes, be content with what you have gained. Stop driving yourself and Ray'. Fortunately I dismissed this conversation from my mind—I knew I could improve. I am sure these friends felt impatient as they watched me try to do very ordinary, every day things, as I tried to gain more independence. Some found this too hard to handle, so stayed away.

Others said, 'I told you so' when I suffered an epileptic type attack. That morning I had dusted and tidied up, in a fashion, as a relative who lived in Brisbane and two friends were breaking their trip to Sydney to have lunch with me. I was excited and looked forward very much to their stop over. To speak with people 'in the world outside' was a rare experience. Perhaps the excitement and anticipation of their visit triggered this attack. I thought I was having another stroke, it was so sudden. I was standing at the kitchen sink washing a few dishes and my son had just dropped in to check on his mum. It came as a flash of warmth and in inner rocking motion. I felt suspended in time for a minute. My son was as frightened by this sudden attack as I and telephoned the doctor. My friends and the doctor arrived at the same time.

The attack passed. I lay on the bed, doctor taking my pulse and periodically checking my blood pressure. He stayed with me until they became stable. On querying him on a reoccurrence of this experience he gave what I consider an honest appraisal of the situation as he saw it—that I might suffer more attacks, but in his opinion they would decrease in severity with longer spacing between attacks, and that is what occurred. I soon recognised a slight aura of warning, which gave me sufficient time to sit down. I learned to relax, to not fight the attack, just flow with it, and to also know it would pass.

I remarked to Ray that after each episode I felt a little different, as though something was unwinding. I never went backwards following an attack.

Since the publication of this book I have talked with many groups in New South Wales, Victoria and Queensland. People who work in large city hospitals, companion services, community caring groups, medical students, people who have had a stroke and also with new stroke families! I hope understanding and changes in attitudes towards stroke people have occurred, and problems have been addressed. Knowledge without action is impotent.

Rebuilding a life

The path of rehabilitation is a long and slow one, and I realise that my friends and family who have stayed beside me during this journey have either a great interest in discovering more about loss of body-image or they love me more than they love themselves. My true friends have included me in social activities as they did in the past. They have walked beside me at a much slower pace. They have made time so that we could pursue together, as in the past, those things we mutually enjoy.

These friendships have taken on new dimensions. There is no pretending any more. If I am tired I say so. If my friends are going somewhere which would be impossible for me to go, they tell me so. This is a mature attitude which I can share. I now have a more honest and caring relationship with people. I have formed new and close friendships with people such as my dear friend Elaine, whom I had met only casually before my stroke.

My husband Ray remained very close throughout this catastrophe of stroke which came upon us without warning. He tried to anticipate my need for help and has done this without exposing me to the very real danger of loss of independence by becoming over-protective. I am sure the strain was very great when he had to stand back and watch me try new and unknown pathways. I am glad he understood my need to regain my independence. He has shown great perception in knowing what to let me do by myself and when to step in with help.

It was only a short time after my discharge from the Physiotherapy Department as an out-patient that I noticed that my shoulder was becoming stiff; in fact, the upper part of the left side of my body felt very heavy. Ray had been giving my leg and arm a nightly massage. By this practice we hoped to stimulate circulation and also keep my muscles in good condition. Ray's fingers also showed me the extremity of the left side of my body. We suddenly realised that we had been neglecting my shoulder. I am not able to shrug it in the normal manner, and I was missing my exercise routine. Now, every morning for a few minutes Ray rotates my shoulder. This practice has made an amazing difference, and if we neglect it for a few days, I find my side and shoulder feeling heavy once more.

It was through interaction with people that a pattern of normality gradually began to appear in our lives. Social interaction began in small ways but one event led to another, and very soon we were going out to dinner and taking in a show or two. Soon a more enjoyable and less restricted life style emerged.

A new year had started, and on that first day of January 1977 I wanted to do something momentous. The day was hot, and it became obvious what that special event would be—a dip in the cool blue waters of Lake Macquarie, which is close to our home. Ray unearthed my swimming costume. I hadn't worn it for quite some time and it was too tight. With perspiration dripping from our faces, we battled to pull my bathing suit up over my hips. This proved to be no simple task, and I felt very hot and frustrated. Ray suggested that I wear my old red shorts and white T-shirt, and by now I was willing to try anything to get to the lake's cool water. It was only a few minutes drive to the lake. We had been there only a short time when family and friends joined us for a picnic.

I stood on the water's edge, closely guarded on both sides by friends. Ray removed my brown lace-up boots, only to discover that I was unable to take even one step without them. How could we have overlooked this important fact? David, the son of one of our friends, came to my rescue with an old pair of desert boots. It was in this attire that I was literally launched into the water. What an experience that was! I was gently lowered into the shallow water by my husband and friends and placed in a sitting position on the pebbly bottom of the lake foreshore. The cool water was exhilarating, but we were all amazed and greatly amused to discover that my left leg refused to stay submerged. There we were, amidst much laughter, trying to anchor my left leg to the bottom of the lake. It was almost as though my left leg was completely independent of the rest of my body and had a mind of its own. However, in due course we decided that if I could be taken out waist-deep I might manage this new situation more easily. Words cannot describe the wonderful feeling of freedom from weight achieved by my first venture into the water. The buoyancy of the water allowed me to enjoy a feeling of weightlessness for the first time since my stroke. The indescribable weight of my left arm was suddenly minimised, and I was able to exercise my arm independently in a way I had not been able to do since my stroke.

I felt supremely happy, and we all decided I must spend very much more time in the water. A means had to be found to keep my foot on the bottom and allow me to concentrate on moving and exercising my left arm. To enjoy this relaxing therapy I needed the feeling of stability. Ray made me an anklet of lead sinkers, the type fishermen use, and although he used many of them, my leg still floated to the surface. When a lead weight used by skin divers was added, my left leg remained submerged. I needed to use this anklet for about two months; after that my leg obeyed my mind.

Having overcome my problems in the water, I now spend much time in deeper water. It took me twelve months to learn to swim again, and eventually I was swimming approximately 500 metres every weekend with an occasional swim during the week. The swimming stroke I use is the Australian crawl (overarm). I had to learn to roll my body in a rhythmical movement so that my shoulder was out of the water; then I was able to lift my arm and bring it forward into the water to complete the stroke. At times I have difficulty in lifting and bringing my arm forward; then I know I haven't rolled over far enough. I would go for a swim every day in the summer if I could find somebody to accompany me. Only once did I go on my own and I was worried the whole time, fearing that a dog or small child might run off with my walking cane. My cane is a necessity when walking on pebbles or rough ground. As my centre of gravity is still moved to the right, I use my cane to recapture my balance when walking on uneven ground.

Therapeutic benefit from swimming is very valuable. For some months Ray had pain in his shoulders, and his arm movements were becoming restricted. This caused us a great deal of worry and concern. By the end of summer, and after he had spent a great deal of time in the water, Ray's arm movements were restored and his pain vanished. From our experience I can thoroughly recommend the value of 'water therapy'.

Having indulged in my 'New Year's whim', and having been so completely amazed at what this had accomplished, I resolved then and there to set the wheels in motion towards other new experiences. The co-operation that I received from my family and friends towards this goal was unbelievable. From this time on we enjoyed the sunshine every weekend: swimming in the lake, walking in the bush, driving in the forests—things that I had expected never to do again. Sometimes it is only our own mental inhibition that limits our experiences. Once I had grasped this vital fact, I used my mind in more positive and constructive ways.

I was hungry for mental stimulation. Friends were encouraging us to accompany them on outings into the country. We went, and I discovered that I was very much at home walking along a bush track. Because I needed to look where I placed my feet, I walked with my eyes cast down, and I saw flowers and grasses that are unnoticed by most people whose eyes are focused on different levels. I gathered some of these treasures of nature so that I could enjoy their beauty a little longer.

Pressing flowers and grasses had been a hobby of mine for many years. My interest was once more stimulated and I realised that I could still pursue this fascinating and creative hobby. Because of my determination to pick a piece of grass, a leaf or a flower that I could see in the distance, my walking skill improved. Sometimes I walked through long grass and over rough ground, even stepping over logs so that I might investigate new miracles of nature. I felt free and alive when I was surrounded by the bushes and trees of the forest. Many times my legs or my pylon became entangled in vines or caught in roots. When this happened to my left leg, I needed assistance to free it. This often meant standing patiently until help arrived. I was never fearful on these occasions and always felt the vines were holding me rather than trying to trip me.

Our set of encyclopaedias started to bulge with the flowers and grasses that I pressed. I began making gift tags, cards and flower pictures. My friends liked them and soon I found myself quite busy producing these to fill the orders placed by my friends who used them as gifts. It was a joy for me to know that I had not lost all of my artistic ability. A friend brought me a beautiful flower press from England, and Ray used it as a pattern to make me several more. The encyclopaedias have gone back to their normal shape and are now used for their original purpose.

The flowers I gathered on the first day that I walked along a bush track are now made into a picture. It hangs on the wall as a reminder to me that 'the best things in life are free'.

In February 1977 we attended a dinner-dance held at the local yacht club. This club is in a beautiful position on the foreshore of Lake Macquarie. From our table we had a magnificent view of the lake. There was a full moon that night and the water sparkled and glistened in the golden light. Surrounded by my family and friends, I felt everything was perfect.

I happened to see a familiar face on the other side of the auditorium: a young man I had known quite well in the last few weeks before I had my stroke. Tony had been a regular visitor to the Occupational Therapy Department where we had been giving him finger exercises to help restore function in his badly cut hand. With Ray beside me and my right hand on my pylon, I walked across the room. Tony and I had a short chat; then Ray and I started to walk back to our table. Just then the band began to play once more. We were quickly surrounded by dancing couples and, worse still, the lights were dimmed. This was great for the dancers but terrible for me. I panicked. I had suddenly lost half of my self. People were moving very quickly on the dance floor, as one would expect. I felt that I had only one leg and, because of this, I didn't know how to take a step. It was with the help, reassurance and calming attitude of my husband that I eventually reached the table.

I was shocked at how quickly an enjoyable night can turn into a nightmare through the sudden loss of body-image I experienced when the lights were dimmed. I still have trouble in walking at dusk when there is half-light; I am actually more capable when it is completely dark. Then I seem to develop another sense which has more to do with feeling and knowing than with seeing. I have had many unusual experiences in the half-light and have long since learned not to panic. If I remain calm I can sort out my problems.

Because a way of life changes, it doesn't mean that it becomes less interesting. It is, however, different from the way we lived our lives before. It is important to understand that people who have lost contact with the left side of their body are not just denying that it exists. It is because of physical damage to the assaulted brain that it is no longer receiving or processing any information about the left side. It is not just a psychological reaction to hemiplegia.

I suffered grief because of my immobility; I was aware of this aspect of my stroke. I felt it happen at the very moment of stroke, but I could not truly grieve until I could look at the left side of my body and claim it as my own, and then to realise I had lost the ability, which I had possessed since birth, to know where my whole body was in space. People do not usually remain grief-stricken forever. The emotion is too strong. They assess what they have and then start to rebuild a life with what remains. A totally new way of living usually occurs. Also a satisfactory mode of being and doing may be evolved from the facilities which are available. The patient who has lost the idea of half of his body needs gentle persuasion and time to understand.

Sexuality and the stroke victim

Although my husband and I had been well advised and informed about how to restructure our home to suit my needs, the important aspect of our sexual future together was not discussed at all. We decided to investigate this for ourselves and found that our ability to love and express our love in sexual satisfaction had not altered because of my stroke. Do you ask whether I experienced half an orgasm? No. It was a whole and complete experience.

In the words of Swami Akhandananada, 'Sex is an undeniable aspect of being human, a reality of all creation. Without its mystery none of us would be here'. Elsewhere he writes, 'Clearly, pleasure is an important aspect of sexuality. The shared enjoyment of intercourse and the intimacy involved can bring a powerful and loving dimension to a relationship. It is foolish to deny the reality of this. By doing so we subject ourselves to numerous suppressions and divisions'. On reading his words, one immediately grasps their significance to rehabilitation in this field as well as in other aspects of living.

We are all human beings, living in a human world. Each of us has a body, and we need physical, emotional and mental stimulation to feel alive. Through primitive language of the body we can convey messages of love, tenderness and affection.

After the intitial crisis following the onset of stroke, the patient often feels great urgency to renew sexual relations with his or her partner. This desire may arise from the stroke victim's need to be reassured that his partner still loves him and is not repulsed by his disablement.

If counselling on sexuality is not given before the patient is discharged from hospital and if he and his partner feel worried and apprehensive about commencing this activity, I would suggest that they consult their doctor and ask if they should take any particular precautions. This will remove some stress from their tender, loving, reunion in which the able-bodied partner may need to use 'every trick in the book' combined with acute awareness, understanding and tenderness to engender once more a feeling of self-worth in his partner. From this a secure and wholesome relationship should evolve.

A commonsense handling of this coming together for the first few times is most important. The able-bodied partner may need to take the active role, thus conserving the energy of his or her mate. They may need to reverse positions for a more relaxed form of body contact. Attention must be paid to any basic discomfort which may be caused by the disabled partner being unable to move his paralysed limbs, or, in the case of a person with perceptual problems, unable to find his limbs. He may feel the pain from an arm or leg that has become trapped in an awkward and unnatural position. It was at times like this that I became panic-stricken, because I had lost touch with my body and its position in space.

The hemiplegic patient may experience heightened reflexes and perhaps contractions in his paralysed limbs. Just moving the position of his leg or arm can sometimes relieve these unwanted distractions which interfere with sexual arousal. In being sensitive to each other's needs, the partners can develop an enjoyable relationship and find momentary release from disablement in the peak of orgasm.

Some case histories of people with whom I have shared experiences:

Joe, aged 68 and a left hemiplegic, had spent six months in a rehabilitation unit after he suffered his stroke. No one in the health team spoke to him or his wife about his sexuality, but he talked to his wife about this very important aspect of their future life together. She recalls vividly his depression when he thought that he would no longer be able to express his deep feelings for her in a physical manner because of having suffered a stroke.

Joe's wife had never taken the initiative in their sexual relationship but she instinctively knew that this would now be her role. The ability to change from a pattern or way of expressing love in a manner in which we feel confident and secure does not come readily to some people. So, 'top marks' go to this gentleman and his lady who were prepared to change so that they could recapture the pleasure that an intimate relationship brings.

Love can be expressed in many ways — cuddling, embracing and touching usually lead to a more intimate encounter.

It was with the gentle touch of warm affection that Joe achieved an erection. He managed to maintain it for only a short time, but during that period he did have an orgasm and he did ejaculate. However, he was unaware of doing so. Joe was very tired after this, his first sexual experience since having his stroke, but he told his wife that the procedure they had followed was very enjoyable to him. He also remarked that tension was released from his body and mind. Their next sexual encounter was much more successful. Joe maintained an erection for much longer and he was more fully aware of his sexuality. This time he knew when he reached the peak of orgasm.

At the time of this report, it is only two months since Joe came home from hospital. Perhaps their love-making is less frequent than it was before, but as Joe laughingly says, 'The quality is as good as ever'. He no longer has any problems in expressing his love and achieving sexual fulfilment.

We must understand that not everyone has strong sexual desires; it is not a great need for everyone. However, to underestimate the power of sex can also cause problems. If we deny that it matters to us, if we ignore the need for sexual satisfaction, then tensions will mount. Sex can be used to release tensions gradually and naturally.

Not all male hemiplegics may be as fortunate as Joe. They may not achieve an erection as readily as he did, but that need not be the end of their sexuality. There are other methods and alternative ways from which they and their partner can find great enjoyment and fulfilment.

When a person suffers a disabling stroke it is not uncommon for them to feel a great loss of self-esteem. Being able to resume a loving, close relationship can be the beginning of restoration of their morale.

Sometimes it is more important for a man to prove his sexual prowess when he returns home from hospital than it was before he suffered his stroke. On occasions this changed and accelerated pattern of sexual activity can be very disconcerting for his partner. Indeed, she may feel that she is living with a 'sex maniac'. Counselling by someone who understands the psychological problems and physical difficulties of a disabled person can be of great value. In talking things over in a relaxed manner with a sexually uninhibited person, obstacles can quite often be overcome and problems solved.

I think of life as energy. If we do not use the energy we have stored in our body, an explosive situation can arise. A number of disabled people are not able to use this energy in a normal way—that is, by physical exertion. They also quite often lack mental stimulation because their disablement has isolated them from people and social or sporting activities that they enjoyed before.

A good sexual relationship may be one way in which they can express themselves fully and thus release the explosive energy from within. If this energy is accumulated and trapped in our body for some time, we may become difficult, angry and generally hard to get along with.

Bert was aged sixty-six when he suffered his stroke and became a left hemiplegic. He spent five months in a rehabilitation hospital where he was given extensive retraining in activities of daily living, and he also learned to walk again by using proven and safe techniques. The whole program was aimed at improving his 'quality of life'.

His wife, Mary, was encouraged to participate in some of the retraining programs so that she would understand methods for managing his disability, thus making it possible for her to encourage and help him with bathing, dressing, getting in and out of bed and on and off the toilet, sitting, standing and walking. All of this was in preparation for when he returned home. Nobody talked to them about their sexuality, and as a result this relationship of long standing almost broke down.

Bert was physically a very disabled man whose self-image was in tatters. Only a few weeks after his return home from hospital he found that sexually he could give quite a good account of himself, in fact, almost as good as before he suffered his stroke. Now it is only human nature to play up our strong points, and this is exactly what Bert did. Mary, his wife, couldn't understand his increased interest in sexuality and couldn't tolerate what seemed to her to be excessive demands. She began locking herself in the spare room at night, with the result that Bert became more frustrated. Mary felt that she was no longer able to cope with this situation. She telephoned the Community Health Services in their area and asked that nursing home accommodation be found for her husband.

A member of the Health Team called to see her and it became apparent that there was certainly something very wrong. Apart from looking very tired, Mary seemed distressed and anxious. She told her visitor that she was no longer able to cope with having her husband at home. Mary was offered additional home-help but she refused it and was quite definite that she wanted Bert 'placed'. On being told that there was quite a long waiting list for most nursing homes, Mary burst into tears. It was only then that she confided in her visitor the real reason for her request. 'He has become a sex maniac', she said.

After lengthy counselling, Mary began to understand her husband's problems and her fear of him diminished. She became eager to co-operate and to encourage him with any suggestions made by their counsellor. This sensitive situation between husband and wife was soon relieved.

Every Tuesday a voluntary driver called for Bert and drove him to a day centre. Bert hadn't really wanted to go there, and it was only after much persuasion that he consented to give it a try. But Tuesday soon became a very important day in his week. It was the day when he met and enjoyed the companionship of other people. Day centres are usually manned by voluntary workers, and Bert found that they not only provided him and his companions with a good lunch, but they brought laughter and happiness into his life as well.

On Thursday of each week Bert was driven by his neighbour to the bowling club, and seated there on the side-line he gained stimulation by watching, and indeed mentally 'playing', each bowl. He was astounded to see a bowler walk onto the green using a walking stick. On looking closely, Bert discovered that the usual rubber on the end of the cane had been replaced with a plumber's friend—a large, black suction cap normally used for cleaning drain pipes and blocked sinks. Not only did the cane leave the green unmarked, but it was able to stand alone because of its large base.

After the match Bert had a long and interesting discussion with the owner of the unusual walking cane. This man had suffered a stroke three years before and he was happy to share his experiences of the past three years with Bert. He became excited when recounting ways he had found and devices he had invented to help him lead a more enjoyable life. This day out with his mates, talking to them over a couple of beers, rejoicing with the winners and commiserating with the losers, and also meeting someone with problems like his own made Bert realise that life could be fun but it was up to him to make it so.

Bert's and Mary's life became more balanced. Mary now had two days a week to pursue her own interests and Bert was much happier because he felt accepted by his mates. He began to feel secure in the society in which he lived.

Olive (aged 57) spent four months in a rehabilitation hospital after she had her stroke. She and her husband, George, now look back and wonder why sexuality was never discussed with them before Olive was discharged from hospital. Because of this they both felt that 'that part' of their life must be over.

The staff at the rehabilitation hospital had always drawn Olive's attention to her strong points and encouraged her to use what she had. Olive and George reasoned that they would surely have been told if this important part of their lives could be resumed. Olive's mother had suffered two strokes before she died and they were worried that Olive might suffer the same fate. Yet they missed the closeness that sexuality, engendered by love, brings to two people, especially in times of trouble.

Because of lack of information these two people were depriving themselves of a loving and natural relationship. Their fear was that sexual activity might cause Olive to have another stroke. Fortunately it was only a few days before their strong feeling for each other overcame their fear.

Their first sexual experience after the stroke was no laughing matter; it was a difficult task rather than a pleasurable experience. Making love was much more complex and intricate than it had been before. They both had to adapt to this 'new' body that lacked rhythm and movement, with only one arm and one leg doing what both had done before. Their bodies were like strangers coming together. They both badly wanted to recapture the warm relationship that they had enjoyed in the past. George kept thinking, 'God, don't let this bring on another stroke'. Olive felt the tension within him and wondered if her altered physical appearance plus lack of body flexibility was 'turning him off'. They both did reach a climax but it was almost with the feeling of, 'Thank goodness that ordeal is over'.

Because they had formed a close and mature relationship before the stroke, they were able to talk about their fears and experiences and decide what to do to alleviate them. They were both aware that books describing different sexual attitudes and positions were available from almost any paper shop, library or bookshop. So they decided to purchase one and 'try another way'.

I have examined other sexual responses both in men and women who have suffered disablement due to hemiplegia, and I have found that a person's sexuality is usually restored to much the same level of involvement and enjoyment as it had reached prior to their disablement.

There are alternative ways of doing most things in life and our sexuality is no exception. If you are seeking some kind of new experience there are many books available on the subject. By reading them you can adapt their suggestions to fulfil your needs and those of your partner.

Some suggested reading:—

The Joy of Sex, edited by Alex Comfort
Sexual Joy and Marriage, Clark and Clark
Advice to Women, Robert Chartham
Husbands and Lovers, Robert Chartham
The Sensuous Couple, Robert Chartham
Sex for Beginners, Robert Chartham

In my opinion counselling on sexuality would enhance any rehabilitation program, for it is by removing barriers and learning alternative techniques that people can overcome fears and resume the natural function of sexuality—coming together in love.

Yoga

One day about eighteen months after having suffered my stroke, I was browsing through a magazine when the word 'yoga' caught my eye. I had always wanted to know more about yoga — not just the exercise part, but the whole concept.

I knew that the time was fast approaching when I would be discharged from the Physiotherapy Department and was aware that I would then have to make my own way. I wondered if yoga could help me. Was it too late? Was yoga only for young and able-bodied people?

It was no use sitting and wondering about this. Past experience had shown me that it is only the present moment that is real. If we do something with the present moment, we make the future happen. By thinking too much in the past, or just day-dreaming of the future without action, we camouflage and hide the present and it is then that we stay still, just dreaming. Action must spring from our ideas, for it is then that we make movement. Life is movement. Death is non-movement. I wanted to live my life more abundantly.

A telephone call to my friend Gwen gave me the information that I required. She assured me that all people can practise yoga, the only requirement being that you want to do so.

Elaine was interested in coming to yoga with me. She had suffered from a kidney complaint for a number of years, and it was not improving. Her doctor was reluctant to increase her drug dosage and he suggested yoga relaxation and meditation as an alternative treatment. Elaine's story is not mine, and only she can tell it; but the difference that can be seen in her whole being is unbelievable. I was delighted to have her company as I ventured into yoga.

Two weeks later we attended our first yoga class. It was a beginners' course which was of twelve weeks' duration. Most of the people there were new to yoga, which gave me something in common with them. But I did feel so different and was very conscious of my disablement. It was so difficult for me to overcome that moment of self-consciousness. I wanted to run away.

This was my first experience of joining in a group activity where I appeared to be the only disabled person. I longed for the protected environment of the Physiotherapy Department where having a difficulty was more usual than unusual. Here, this night, everyone had changed their body position from standing to sitting on the floor without giving it a thought. I stood there wondering how to go about making this very difficult manoeuvre. Our yoga teacher suggested that I might prefer to carry out my practices seated on a chair. I declined, as I felt that would only accentuate the difference between me and the others.

The chair that had been so kindly brought to me I used for leaning on and, remembering all of my training from the past, I very carefully lowered myself on to my yoga mat. It was the first time that I had done this without someone standing beside me. A habit I had developed from the time I had my stroke was to hold my breath when doing something that was difficult for me. Little did I know how important breath awareness is. My therapist used to say, 'Take a breath, Lorna; you are going blue in the face!'

I lifted my head expecting to find many pairs of eyes turned on me with pity, and I was relieved to see most people lying on their yoga mats with their eyes closed. Those who were watching were not doing so with pity. They were just watching with awareness in case I needed their help. What flights of fancy we take because we feel sorry for ourselves! I felt pity for myself, but could not face this fact so changed it to: 'I can't bear other people to feel sorry for me'.

Our yoga teacher was a young man. Peace flowed from him. His manner was quiet and yet he spoke with authority. He sat so easily in the position of *padmasana* (lotus) and he quietly talked to us of many things. When he told us that the meaning of the word 'yoga' is yoke or union, I knew that was what I was seeking. Union between my body, mind and spirit. My body and mind had little communication taking place between them, and the fear and trauma caused by this was burying my spiritual self deeper and deeper. He talked to us about the difference between exercise as we had known it (something that was strenuous and required all our strength) and the yoga postures, which are carried out in a relaxed and effortless manner. There was to be no holding the breath. He too had noticed my bad habit.

He said most people realise that excessive stress can cause disease in the body or mind. Through yoga practices, the harmful effects of stress can be reduced. He ended his talk by saying, 'If you practise yoga regularly every day, a change will take place in your life'. I was looking forward to a big change taking place in mine.

He demonstrated some simple yoga *asanas* (postures) and then led us into first one and then another. He emphasised natural breathing at all times, not holding your breath as I was wont to do. Just gently and slowly, using no force, we proceeded to learn our first yoga postures. There were few that I was able to complete. I did what I could in my own funny way and then watched the others, hoping that I might learn by mental rehearsal. I watched carefully and then closed my eyes and endeavoured to carry out mentally what I was unable to do physically. Over the weeks I progressed by using this method that had already been so useful to me in the past. He then asked us to lie down on our backs on our yoga mats, palms upward, which is the pose of relaxation. The next instruction was to become aware of the breath in our nostrils. I was so insensitive I couldn't even feel the breath in my own nostrils. We were told it would be cold when we inhaled and warmer as it passed out through our nostrils.

It was quite some time before I was able to witness this very natural phenomenon of feeling the breath in my own nostrils. I had not realised that I had become so out of touch with my own body, and I decided then and there that even if I could never ably do my postures there were so many, many things that I would learn from yoga.

Our first lesson ended with relaxation (yoga nidra) which was followed by a short guided meditation. For the practice of yoga nidra we lay down on our mats in the pose of relaxation. The lights were turned off; then we were asked to close our eyes. I closed mine and then they snapped open again. I became alarmed because of being unable to see my whole body.

Instructions commenced: make sure that your head and spinal column are straight (I didn't know what straight was unless I was able to see); palms of your hands facing upwards. (I knew where my right hand was and that my palm was facing upwards but I couldn't locate my left hand at all.) I panicked; here I was in the dark, feeling like a caged animal wanting to run from this, yet another situation that was uncomfortable to me. I was dismayed that I was unable to follow these simple instructions.

Fortunately, the next directive I *was* able to carry out: listen to the outside sounds. We were directed to just listen to all of the different sounds outside the building. First the close sounds, perhaps the footsteps of somebody walking along the pavement, a dog barking, the sound of a cricket singing, leaves rustling on a nearby tree. Then we were asked to move our awareness to more distant sounds. Our teacher asked us just to become aware of the sound and listen to it for a few moments and then pass on to the next sound. He said this was not an intellectual exercise. We were just to use the faculty of hearing. This practice I could carry out with a great degree of success; also the next, which was to be aware of my own breath by mentally saying, 'I am breathing in, I am breathing out'. Once more, breath awareness was helping me as it had in the first few days of my illness to find some measure of relaxation. He then suggested that we make a resolve. A positive goal to aim towards. Something that we really wanted to happen in our lives. I had been making these positive suggestions to myself for some time and I knew what I wanted to happen in my life, so I made my resolve accordingly.

Our next direction was to become aware of our whole body lying on the floor, to feel the parts of our body that were making contact with the floor. Although I was only aware of the right side of my body, I was glad that I now had the realisation that my left side did exist somewhere out there. I was unable to locate where. I no longer wanted to run away and was feeling relaxed from our previous practices. Swami Poornananda, our teacher, then said he would lead our consciousness to different parts of the body and he told us to be alert but not to concentrate too intently; just develop awareness and repeat mentally the names of the different parts of our bodies and try to move our minds as quickly as possible as instructed by him. 'Do not sleep' was an instruction that was repeated at regular intervals.

I followed his instructions and rotated my awareness, commencing with my right thumb and continuing up my right arm and then down the whole of the right side of my body, ending with my right toes. Then our rotation of awareness was drawn to our left sides. I was unable to locate any part of the left side of my body. I had been taught to find and use the left side of my body by using my eyes. Now I was unable to follow the instructions because it was dark. I knew that I had to beat this moment of despair. I had been there before and knew that the moment would pass, as other unpleasant ones had in the past. I knew that if I couldn't do this I would stay immobilised and make no further progress. That moment did pass. I lay there on my yoga mat and just listened to his voice and let time pass. A guided meditation followed and then our first yoga class came to a close.

There were many questions in my mind, but in my heart I knew that I had indeed found a truth in yoga. I asked many questions during the first few weeks that we attended yoga classes, but it was not the answers to any of my questions that enabled me to make progress. It was by following the advice given by our yoga teacher. 'Do not become discouraged if you cannot carry out every instruction perfectly', he said. 'Just relax and enjoy doing them; but do them every day because it is by regular daily practice that a change will take place in your life.' He advised us to adjust our practices to the time we had available. Fifteen minutes each day is better than two hours twice a week, was the advice that he gave.

He told us to be aware at all times and never to let our practices become automatic and mindless. It was this system of total awareness of my every action, coupled with regular daily exercises, simple breath awareness and yoga nidra that brought about such a change in my life.

My daily yoga practices, lasting about half an hour, were as follows. I lay on my back and closed my eyes, then relaxed my body and mind by becoming aware of the breath in my nostrils. I counted each breath. Starting from twenty-seven, I counted backwards to one. It was by keeping my mind occupied in this manner that I was able to achieve a state of relaxation in quite a short time. It was most important for me to allow all tension to flow out of my body before commencing my exercise program.

I came to a sitting position with my legs directly in front of my body. Until my back muscles strengthened, I found it necessary to sit with my back against a wall. I repeated all exercises five times if I felt comfortable doing this, but if I felt too much strain I reduced the number of times to three. It was most important for me to remember that my life was to change from tension and stress to relaxation.

Exercise 1. Total awareness of my toes; moving them slowly forward and backward.

Exercise 2. Ankle bending—I moved the whole of my right foot backwards and forwards, bending from the ankle joint and keeping my knee straight. My awareness was centred on my ankle joint. I repeated this exercise mentally with my left foot. I watched it in a relaxed manner and with hope that perhaps one day a pattern of movement might appear.

Exercise 3. Ankle rotation—keeping my heel in contact with the floor, I rotated my right foot clockwise and then anti-clockwise. I was unable to do this with my left foot so did it mentally.

Exercise 4. Ankle crank—I placed my right ankle on my left thigh and tried to hold it there with my left hand, but the hand kept letting go of my toes and would fall by my side. I helped it with my right hand and together my hands would rotate my foot, first clockwise then anti-clockwise. Each time I did this my left hand assumed more responsibility for the movement. Although my awareness should have been centred on my ankle, I found it necessary to concentrate on my hand holding my foot. The benefit that I received from this exercise was certainly in my arm and hand. In a few short weeks I had much greater control over them.

Exercise 5. Knee bending—I clasped my hands under my right thigh, then bent the right leg as much as possible at the knee and then straightened my leg, keeping my heel off the floor. I was able to repeat part of this exercise with my left leg and in a short time greatly improved the movement. This exercise was also beneficial for my left arm and improved my balance.

Exercise 6. Body twist—I separated my legs as much as possible and endeavoured to bring my left hand to my right toes, take my right arm straight out behind me, then turn my head and twist my body and look backwards at my right hand. This was by far the most difficult exercise and I assumed some most peculiar postures when I first tried to repeat it with my left hand at the back. I did gradually improve and found this exercise also improved my balance.

Exercise 7. Hand clenching—holding my arm straight out in front at shoulder height and parallel to the floor, palm facing down, I first stretched my fingers right out and then closed them, making a tight fist. This is done slowly and with complete awareness. When I tried to repeat this with my left hand, it was necessary to support my arm with my right hand. I now no longer need to give this support.

Exercise 8. Wrist bending—holding my arm straight out in front as in the previous exercise, I bent my right hand at the wrist, turning my palm outward as though I was pressing against a wall. Then I bent my hand downwards so that my palm was facing towards me. I needed to support my left arm with my right hand when first doing this exercise, but now I no longer find this necessary.

Exercise 9. Wrist rotation—arm as in previous position. I rotated my hand first clockwise and then anti-clockwise. Once more I needed to support my arm with my right hand.

Exercise 10. Elbow bending—maintaining the same position with arm outstretched and palm facing upwards, I bent my right arm and brought my fingers to my shoulder. I then straightened my arm again. On trying to repeat this exercise with my left hand I was unable to find my shoulder. I am more able to do this now.

Exercise 11. Shoulder socket rotation—I assumed the same position. With my right hand resting on my right shoulder I made a circular movement with my elbow, making as wide a circle as possible—first clockwise, then anti-clockwise, slowly and with complete awareness. On repeating this movement with my left arm, I needed to hold my hand on my shoulder with my right hand. I still need to do this.

The last exercise was neck movements, and they entailed rolling my head first to one side, then the other, letting it fall forward on to my chest and then backward, followed by a minimum amount of head rotation, as this caused me to become giddy.

These were very much the same exercises that were taught at William Lyne Hospital. However, at the yoga classes emphasis was placed on relaxation and awareness. Becoming relaxed before commencing my exercises and carrying them out slowly and with complete awareness certainly produced much quicker and greater results. I consider that learning to relax mind and body should be placed very early on the list of any rehabilitation scheme. By learning to move with awareness a whole new and interesting world was revealed to me, that world being my own body. I had resided in it since birth and yet knew so little about it. Undoubtedly as a child I had known much more. Now it was with interest and awareness that I watched my movements, just as a baby does when it first discovers its hands and feet. I wanted to recapture this childlike quality so that I could learn, as I had then, by awareness. On completion of my physical exercises I lay on my mat once more in the pose of relaxation. I watched my breath until I was breathing quietly and evenly and then continued my practices with some simple, but very effective, breathing exercises.

Breath awareness always has a very calming effect on me; just two or three minutes of simple breath awareness and I can feel composed and relaxed in a situation in which I had felt tense before, and when this happens, what was difficult becomes easy. This I followed by a short meditation. These practices took half an hour to complete, the most important half-hour of the day, for it was from carrying them out with regularity each day and attending my yoga class once a week that a great change took place in me. Bitterness and fear that had produced inner tension started to melt away. I can only liken it to a 'spring cleaning' of my mind, getting rid of all the junk to leave space for new ideas and insights. I looked up the word 'insight' in our dictionary. It means 'to have sight into something, an immediate perception of the truth'. It is not memory, not knowledge, not an idea. It is a knowing. I knew that since I had started practising yoga a deep meaningful knowing about myself had been growing. I knew that I knew I was more than I was. I can't explain this because it has nothing to do with intellect.

Gradually I found that I was becoming more aware of the left side of me—not however, as I knew the right side. My left side was more like a shadow. This shadow first appeared during yoga nidra when I was in a very relaxed state, and I found the more relaxed I became, the more the shadow became defined and solid. It was something like having a sketchy plan to work from. I am still trying to get the correct layout of my left side, but happily most of it is now complete in my mind.

Our twelve-weeks yoga course came to an end, but another beginners' course commenced the following week. Many of us decided to repeat the course and were joined by friends and, I am delighted to say, my husband Ray. It was so good to share this experience with him. I was no longer a 'new chum' and was delighted when I realised how far I had come since that first night. Two and a half years have passed since I first started to practise yoga, and I now realise that true relaxation only takes place when you find something that is meaningful in your life: something that you can become at one with. It may be music, drama, art, God or some form of religion, or a host of other things. It must be something to which you can give your devotion. If it is music, then you become one with the music. When this happens, your life comes into focus. Relaxation and meditation take place. You can find yourself by losing yourself in something that is totally meaningful to you. Your involvement with stress ceases, the creative you that has been supressed emerges, and you become the unique *you* that you were born to be.

However, if you are in ill health and decide to practice yoga, do consult your doctor first. Find yourself a good yoga teacher and inform him of any precautions that your doctor has advised you to take. In this chapter I have only described very briefly some of the practices that helped me. For several months I had private classes. Because of my gross perceptual problems (unawareness of my left side) my teacher changed my practices so that the emphasis was on my left side. He also guided me in visualisations that undoubtedly made me much more aware of everything to the left of me.

Quite recently I read the words of Hsun Tzu: 'Man's mind can be compared to water; when still its dust drops to the bottom and the water becomes clear on the surface. Only then can the realities of our figures be reflected in it. When a light, gentle wind passes over the water, the dirt is stirred up and beclouds the surface. As a result, the reality of things is not then reflected. So is the mind . . . if it is obscured by externals, it does not discern between falsity and truth'.

It is necessary for me to find that stillness in my mind at least once every day, so my yoga practices have become a very necessary part of my life. Everyone must find their own joys within themselves. Knock on your own inner door. It was yoga that lead me to that door.

Fine tuning

The doctor of the future will give no medicine, but will interest his patient in the care of the human frame, in diet, and in the cause and prevention of disease.
Thomas A. Edison (1847 - 1931)

Quite often people are not offered the same service that is automatically given to the family car. I believe that many people are discharged from hospital without 'fine tuning' being attended to, and some leave hospital without a referral or information about where they may receive treatment from people who specialise in this field.

Most car owners demand fine tuning for their car and will repeatedly return it to the mechanic if it is not running well. The car owner has no qualms about doing this until the fine tuning has been properly attended to or until he has been referred to a 'specialist'. Why then don't we seek specialists in fine tuning for ourselves or our loved ones who are flesh and blood?

It is indeed fine tuning that gives us more potential. I have thought quite a lot about this aspect, one that I believe to be so sadly neglected and not talked about by health professionals involved in rehabilitation of disabled people.

'Fine tuners' within the realms of orthodox medicine include occupational and physiotherapists, dietitians, psychologists, and others. My own general health has improved so much because of fine tuning. This commenced after I was discharged from hospital and when I began attending occupational and physiotherapy departments as an outpatient. I was not automatically referred for outpatient treatment on my discharge from hospital. It was necessary for me to seek a referral for myself. It was our family doctor who, when I asked him, furnished me with that precious slip of paper, my referral to outpatients for ongoing treatment.

Yoga is yet another wonderful form of fine tuning. Daily massage of my arm, shoulder and leg by my husband was, for me, another. There are many and varied methods of massage being used today. I have found it most interesting to acquaint myself with some of these. I feel sure that there are many 'natural therapies' worthy of investigation.

Anything new that has been discovered or invented, any new technique that has been devised, has only come about because someone has dared to be different and has stepped outside already tried and conventional methods to try another way.

An important lesson that I have learned in the last few years is to listen carefully to my own inner voice, and then ponder about the resources within myself and wonder how to set up conditions so that something more is likely to occur. It is something like finding another level from which to move. I realise that we must walk in our own shoes and leave others to walk in theirs, to find their own level and directions.

Through regular yoga practices my posture was greatly improved, but there was room for more improvement. After all, I had been walking with a peculiar gait for well over four years. I realised that my spinal column might indeed need attention.

Chiropractic was a new concept in health care to me and I did not know of anyone who had suffered a stroke and had gone to a chiropractor for treatment. But I did have several friends with other conditions causing discomfort and pain who had gained relief from chiropractic treatment. I read booklets and brochures and talked to people about this treatment and I found that there were many unbiased researchers and doctors who had discerned merit in chiropractic.

In due course, I had a consultation with a chiropractor, one reputed to be highly skilled in her profession and a member of the Australian Chiropractic Association. I found her proficient and caring and quite well informed about my particular type of stroke. She was interested in my condition and totally aware of me as a person. She made no outlandish claims of miracle cures but felt that treatment could give me more potential. She paid me the courtesy of explaining to me her proposed treatment and the results that she hoped to achieve.

Gentle corrective manipulations did achieve results far beyond our expectations. After the first treatment I was able to turn my head and see my left shoulder for the first time since my stroke. Because of this I was more aware of my body position in space. After the next treatment I became aware of the location of my left buttock. For the first time since my stroke I was able to sit down and feel both sides of my bottom on the chair. This was quite an emotional moment for both my chiropractor and myself. My leg now feels different and somehow more secure. As yet, and because of my loss of body-image, I am unable to say why this is so. The benefits that I have already gained have made my chiropractic treatment well worthwhile.

Over the last five years I have met many people who, like me, have suffered a stroke. Several have been people I myself had helped to care for before I suffered the same fate. Some of these people have made progress far beyond the expectations of staff when they were discharged from hospital. After congratulating them on their great progress, I have also questioned them about the reasons for their success. Two facts have emerged. First these people were always highly motivated and had achieved success in some field before their stroke. (Was it because they *expected* to be successful in their efforts to regain independence that they achieved so much?) Second, they sought of their own accord ongoing treatment after being discharged from either the hospital or the outpatients' department and received this treatment from both orthodox and 'natural' therapists. They did not give up.

One small step

Over the years Ray and I had made many plans for our retirement. At the time of my stroke, and for a long time afterwards, it seemed to both of us that our cherished dreams were quite beyond the realm of possibility. It was just one small, wooden step that made it possible to fulfil many of our dreams.

In July 1981 Ray retired. One month later we celebrated our fortieth wedding anniversary by trading our very reliable and well-cared-for station wagon for a second-hand, fitted out VW Campervan. It had taken Ray only an hour or so to build a small, sturdy, portable wooden step. That step made it possible for me to enter the van by the front door and sit in the seat beside him. The step bridged the gap.

The same rule still applied. The rule of finding the right level, or finding a way of bridging the gap. This is a Golden Rule to remember; it is the path to more freedom and independence.

This new vehicle gave plenty of leg-room. I found the upright position of the seat less tiring when travelling long distances. My back was well supported, and it was easy to keep my feet in a comfortable, flat position on the floor of the van. The van was now our only means of transport. We used it for shopping and for visiting friends. It was important to use it in the way we had always visualised it: to see more of this beautiful country, Australia, and to pursue a hobby we had both grown to love. Dabbling with paint and brush on canvas had become a delightful and relaxing pastime. Ray, a commercial artist by profession, had had very little time for painting since my illness.

I was a beginner. I had started painting about eighteen months before when some friends asked me to join a small, local art group. They were delightful people and fun to be with, and I became hooked on painting.

In early September, with fingers and toes crossed and offering up a silent prayer to Him above, Ray packed the van and we set forth on our first trip. It was springtime. The weather was divine. We slowly made our way towards the Queensland border. We stayed a few days here, and a few days there, stopping when the mood took us, getting out paints and brushes, trying to capture the feeling of spring on our canvas and, indeed, within ourselves. All around us the trees and wildflowers were coming to life after the long, cold winter.

We found it hard to believe that we actually had time to stop and drink in all of the beauty. We travelled at a leisurely pace, turning off the main highway onto dirt roads which quite often led to delightful places we had never seen before.

On this trip we stayed at some quite small caravan parks, off the main route, and enjoyed the quietness and solitude of the bushland settings. The amenities blocks at the caravan parks where we stayed were well equipped and I had little difficulty in managing my showers. I was relieved to find built-in wooden seats installed in the drying area of shower cubicles, also plenty of hooks from which to hang clothes, towels and, of course, my walking stick. This was an area where we anticipated I might have problems, but few occurred.

I would strongly advise disabled people to personally check the amenities block before booking in to a caravan park. If it doesn't meet their individual needs they should not keep the reason to themselves but tell the proprietors why they cannot stay in the park. Unless we are prepared to tell people, they will never know of the value of quite simple 'props' that are important for our safety when showering and drying ourselves in unfamiliar surroundings and with no husband or wife within calling distance.

If seats and small hand-bars, on which to steady oneself, were installed in appropriate positions in shower recesses and drying cubicles, it would be much easier and safer for disabled and aged people to use the caravan parks of Australia.

We crossed the Queensland border a week after leaving home. In the past we had taken less than two days to travel the same distance. We took two weeks to wend our way home. We called at places we had left out on our way north: little sheltered bays and rivers, hiding at the ends of bumpy dirt roads, were a joy to find and are some of our favourite places. It was in such places that we would unpack our painting gear and stay for a few days, putting down on canvas our impressions of the beauty that surrounded us.

The trip was a great success. Our family and friends were relieved when we arrived home safe and sound, and we were happy and eager to plan another trip. Then, in November 1981 we planned and booked a tour of New Zealand. We spent hours with a travel agent, discussing ways and means of accomplishing the trip. Needless to say the questions asked by me were: How could Ray manage our luggage and also help me when transferring from domestic to international air terminals? Would the tour coach have a portable step? Could I book the front seat behind the coach driver to give me more room for my legs?

The travel agent was remarkably patient and had a store of knowledge in answer to my many questions. I had remembered a conversation with my friend Chris. She had alerted me to the ready availability of wheelchairs for disabled people at airports, and I asked the travel agent that this service be made available for me.

WHEELCHAIR was written on all our plane tickets. Ray and I were astounded at the thoroughness with which our request was carried out. There was not one slip-up. Always a wheelchair and an attendant to take care of me, leaving Ray free to carry out other necessary procedures.

The fact of wheelchair availability at airports should be given more publicity through travel brochures, newspaper advertisements, day-care centres and physiotherapy and occupational therapy departments of hospitals. Some disabled people may not know of services that make it possible for them to travel in a civilised and stress-free manner. Disabled people are well catered for and taken care of at air terminals.

We had three and a half glorious weeks holidaying in New Zealand. Bad weather followed us but didn't catch us. Again it was just one step that made the impossible possible. I was able to climb in and out of a tour coach six or seven times a day for three weeks. That one portable step carried on the coach allowed me to see and do things I had not dreamed possible with my disability.

I wanted to take the light plane which landed on the Tasman Glacier and to actually walk on the glacier itself. It was one small portable, wooden step which once again made the impossible possible. The step bridged the gap and allowed me to get aboard the plane and enjoy the exquisite sights of snow and ice. Our little plane climbed to an altitude of 2000 metres to land on the Tasman Glacier. The step that had been nursed by Ray during our flight was now planted firmly on the glacier. I alighted, followed by three fellow-travellers. Standing and walking on this bed of ice was an unbelievable experience. The beauty of white snow and blue ice surrounding us was quite breathtaking. We had a snow fight and all took photographs. Then it was time to board the plane again. Tom, our pilot, said that to the best of his knowledge it was the first time a step such as mine had been on the Tasman Glacier. What a pity; I hope it isn't the last time.

A little later on our trip, when we arrived at Wellington Airport to meet our new coach driver, Alec, there was no portable step with the coach. Ray and I explained to Alec the important part the step had played in our tour of the South Island. Next morning he produced the funniest little step I have ever seen. We think he made it himself. It was certainly put together in a hurry and was made of rough undressed timber but was very strong and sturdy.

With the help of that step I travelled by coach over much of the North Island. One highlight of the trip was a drive for over sixty kilometres along the broad expanse of Ninety Mile Beach. Saltwater spray fanned out as our wheels skimmed along the sand, which was as hard as cement. We stopped at intervals to gather shells. Shoes and socks were discarded by people who dug for shellfish in the wet sand at the water's edge.

I did not remove my shoes and socks, but I did walk on the beach, and when I arrived back at the bus my pockets were bulging with beautiful shells that had been washed on to the beach from the Tasman Sea. Those shells are now nestling on a cane tray in my home together with shells gathered over the years from beaches on the east coast of Australia.

Without my funny little step I could not have joined in the fun. I would have stayed in the bus feeling miserable and disabled. For each individual there are many ways of 'bridging the gap'. Just one step opened up a whole new world for me.

Afterword: From the other side of the blanket

Just a few days before my discharge from hospital, I was introduced to a trained nurse who had recently joined the Education Team at William Lyne Hospital. She had her diploma in education and was extremely interested to hear the stroke patient's story. She wanted to become more aware of the problems confronting, and indeed confounding, the stroke patient.

These discussions, which began when I was in hospital, continued in my own home when I was discharged a few days later. On these occasions when we talked, time would fly. Lee would just pop in for a few minutes but would invariably stay for an hour or more. She put many and varied questions to me, and I also asked many of her.

Our times together proved to be the beginning of learning for both of us. When two people who are intensely interested in a subject investigate it together, information of great value can be unearthed. This deep communication between the patient and members of the health team is vital to enable the steady advancement of learning to take place.

Lee asked me some eight months later to speak with students who were attending a program in the Education Centre at William Lyne Hospital—the same hospital where I had worked before my stroke as a technical assistant in occupational therapy and where, after having suffered a stroke, I became a patient for the last six weeks of my hospitalisation. In this hospital I was now to share my experience with students.

This was, indeed, to be just the beginning of my participation in teaching. Two years later I was officially invited to join the William Lyne Education Team and, on a casual basis, lecture to students concerning the stroke patient's view from the other side of the blanket.

Students who attend these programs at William Lyne Hospital include medical students, trained nurses, nursing aides, nursing assistants, community nurses and some occupational and physiotherapists. These students come from all types of institutions and services. They are attached to hospitals and nursing homes in Newcastle as well as country areas in the Lower and Upper Hunter Valley. Others come from as far north as Tweed Heads and west to Dubbo. Students from the Hunter Regional School of Nursing, as well as trained nurses doing a post graduate course at Concord Repatriation Hospital, have also attended these lectures.

Administrators or directors of nursing in some country hospitals who realise the isolation of their staff from large teaching hospitals have asked for programs on rehabilitation to be presented in their own hospitals, as staff shortages prevent their nurses from attending planned programs at William Lyne. I have participated in many of these teaching sessions and have become keenly aware of the feeling of sharing with and caring for the total family that prevails in country hospitals. This feeling is not easily expressed in a large city hospital.

My first experience with students in a sharing and teaching capacity was traumatic. I completely relived those terrible weeks after my stroke in order to share my experiences with the students. I was angry when I talked of unremitting pain and the staff's apparent unawareness of my need for help, as well as the lack of information given to me and my family about my type of stroke and what could be done to help me try to understand this trauma.

The fact that the patient is unaware of his loss of body-image is a concept which students find difficult to grasp. So did I—and so do I—because the mind considers that the body is whole: that half is whole.

Eventually I realised that it was not the staff's lack of caring which made me feel they were unaware of my needs. I began to see that they themselves lacked knowledge and information about my type of stroke. It was then that my anger was replaced by a burning desire to help research this little understood and almost totally undocumented area of stroke.

My talks with students have been received with intense interest. For many it was their first opportunity to hear the patient's story and to ask questions of a person who, before her stroke, had been actively involved for six years in the retraining of stroke patients.

Students have often been able to bring to mind patients they have nursed in the past, or stroke patients they are at present nursing and, in the light of our talks together, to understand the hidden problems and ways of helping these people.

Feelings of guilt on the part of nursing staff have been apparent at times, mainly when they realised they had formerly not understood the perceptual sensory and even physical problems associated with stroke. For example, bowel care—or lack of it. The students' disbelief at the neglect of this physical dysfunction was so great that a senior lecturer on the Health Team often had to verify the facts as shown on my chart to be accurate.

Students have spoken about the inadequate amount of information available in written form about the 'twilight world' that some left hemiplegics are allowed to remain in. It is indeed not only in the paramedical field that more information is required, but in other areas as well. Family education is vitally important. Community health workers who establish day-care centres and the volunteers who staff them need to be aware that the stroke person's problems are not only the obvious ones: there are many more hidden problems which need clarification. The Hunter Regional Division of the Health Commission of N.S.W., aware of this, has quite often asked me to address groups of people who work in day-care centres.

Following on requests from a medical practitioner, I have frequently visited and talked with patients suffering from strokes similar to mine. Some of the other groups I have lectured include: the Central Coast Community Health Services Staff Development Programme; several retirement villages; the National Orthopaedic Conference in Sydney; View Clubs at

Dubbo and Wellington; and the Handicapped Association of Redland Bay District in Queensland.

It is at the repeated request of hundreds of students, health professionals, patients and their families that I have written this book.

Postscript

I no longer need to wear lace-up boots, indeed my footwear has been completely updated. What were my best shoes are now my bush walking shoes—solid, heavy and laced up high on my feet.

When I want to be completely independent I use my walking cane—adventuring out alone on previously untried ground and unexplored territory, to ascend and descend stairs that have no hand rail. When I use my walking cane, I can go just about anywhere.

Progress out of stroke for me has been on-going. I continue to improve.

I know again the left side of me and the world around me to the left. My mind has captured what was lost to it before. The left and right sides of my body have merged. I am whole.

My left knee and some of the toes on my left foot are 'dumb', they don't 'speak' to me, but I know they are there and part of me. Improvement is still continuing in these two areas and I expect it to continue.

Each day I spend some time, perhaps only a few minutes, in a mythical, magic place of my own, imagining. Here I can be and do all things. Touch the mind, and the body is also touched and changed in some small way.

I don't have to be super physical to be useful, to be needed and loved.

Perhaps I am in a better position today than ever before in my life, to be in tune with myself, with other people and the world around me.

To be alive and aware is: to love, laugh, listen and just have time to share with others; to work with interest and discipline towards improving my well-being; to take responsibility for my health and my life by watchfulness of what I eat and drink, and by daily exercise in the form of 'movement with awareness', of breath awareness, and by carrying out a relaxation programme each day; and to know that it is up to me to be happy or sad. I alone have the power to make this decision.

I miss spontaneous living—'doing' without conscious thought and planning. Sometimes I slip back into old patterns, but that is all right. It is part of change, change that is taking place within me.

Before I had a stroke I did not appreciate the joy and beauty of co-ordinated movement—the result of silent, unobtrusive and harmonious communication between mind and body, the very basis of action. Because of 'loss' I was better able to understand what was lost.

If I grieve for anything it is for spontaneity of movement.

Stroke Class

I first became aware of stroke clubs when I received a letter from Anita Rosenberg, New South Wales president of the Straight Talk and Stroke Class, congratulating me on the publication of 'When Half is Whole'.

Anita had suffered a stroke at a very young age. Her stroke was in the left brain—she had no speech, could not read or write, and had a marked weakness in the right side of her body. Her mind was very active, yet she could not communicate to her family her feelings and ideas about how she could learn to speak again.

When she returned home from hospital she found the days long—her husband at work, her children at school.

She was very, very lonely.

Anita realised there must be other people in a similar position as herself and the concept of the formation of a group for aphasic people was born—a self-help support group.

Anita travelled to England with her husband Alan and they did the rounds of already established groups. She still had little speech and Alan became spokesperson, as they had found a way of communicating with each other. They longed for the day when Anita could speak for herself.

They became increasingly aware of the shortage of speech pathologists in Australia. Until this gap was bridged they felt they must form groups for stroke victims to help each other. A speech pathologist from a major hospital was interested in this concept and assisted Anita in establishing the first group.

Anita became aware that all strokes were different, that there were other problems associated with stroke apart from loss of or difficulty with speech.

The name of the group was changed from Straight Talk Club to Straight Talk and Stroke Club. This group was recognised by the New South Wales Government. As a responsible and important resource centre they received a small grant of money from Youth and Community Services which enabled them to establish a head office and also to employ a part-time secretary. Their head office is now known as Stroke Recovery Centre and the groups are known as Straight Talk and Stroke Clubs. There are now 21 branches in N.S.W. and the members number over 700.

New groups are being formed all the time. For an update on location of stroke clubs contact The Stroke Recovery Centre, Cleveland House, 1 Bedford St., Surry Hills N.S.W. 2010. Phone (02) 699 4096.

Straight Talk and Stroke Clubs are social and self-help clubs for stroke persons and their families.

Stroke Recovery Centres

Head Office:

Cleveland House
1 Bedford St.
Surry Hills N.S.W. 2010

New South Wales Branches:

Group Meetings
All inquiries ring Head Office (02) 699 4096.

Auburn	10.00 a.m. Friday
	Presbyterian Church Hall, Queen St.
Blacktown	10.00 a.m. Monday
	Blacktown Workers' Club, Campbell St.
Bondi Junction	10.30 a.m. Wednesday
	Bondi Junction—Waverley RSL Club, Gray St.
Chatswood	11.00 a.m. the first Friday of the month
	The Doherty Community Centre, 7 Victoria St.
Forestville	9.30 a.m. Wednesday
	Forestville RSL Club, Melwood Ave.
Haberfield	11.00 a.m. Friday
	Woodfield Lodge, 51-56 Parramatta Rd.
Hills District	Fortnightly
	Anglican Retirement Village, Dover Hall
Hillsdale	11.30 a.m. Monday
	Hillsdale Community Information Centre, Bunnerong Rd.
Lakemba	10.00 a.m. Wednesday
	St John's Bowling Club, Sproule St.

Southern Suburbs	1.00 p.m. Thursday Uniting Church Hall, 181 Rocky Point Rd., Ramsgate
South West	10.30 a.m. Tuesday Neighbourhood Centre, 7 Beale St., Georges Hall

Country Centres (NSW)

Central Coast	Every first Thursday at RSL Club, Gosford
Cootamundra	The first Wednesday of the month Cootamundra Retirement Village
Grafton	Every second Wednesday 10.00 a.m. Community Health Centre, 55 Fitzroy St.
Hawkesbury	Every second Wednesday Richmond Sports Centre
Illawarra	First Thursday of the month Bulli RSL Club
Penrith	2.30 p.m. the fourth Saturday of the month Community Centre
Springwood	Every second Saturday of the month Masonic Hall, Macquarie St.
Taree	Twice monthly St. John's Anglican Church Hall, Victoria St.
Toronto	10.00 a.m. Monday Toronto Workers Club, James St. Call Lorna Hewson on (049) 59 1836
Wagga Wagga	
Port Kembla	Held at the Forest Centre
Coffs Harbour	Coffs Harbour Hospital

Associated Stroke clubs

The Stroke Recovery Association of NSW, Inc
Thomas Street, Lewisham
Postal Address PO Box 673
Petersham 2049
ph (02) 550 0594

Hunters Hill	Each Friday morning Montefiore Nursing Home
Newcastle	New Ways, contact Hunter Volunteer Department Centre 24 Stewart Ave., Hamilton (049) 69 5552
NSW Hunter Region	Hunter Outreach Stroke Recovery Centre Woodrising Neighbourhood Centre Haydenbrook Road Booragul 2284

PO Box 105 Booragul 2284 ph (02) 59 6990 |

Other States

Queensland	S.A.S.S.Y. P.O. Box 156, Manly, 4179
Victoria	B.R.A.S.S. Stroke Recovery Centre, Geelong

Caulfield Hospital: Speech Pathology

Dept. Veterans' Affairs, GPO Box 87A, Melbourne, 3001. Contact Social Worker

Straight Talk and Stroke Club, Kingston Centre, Cheltenham: Contact Nancy Ziegenbein, 14 Allnutt Parade, Cheltenham, 3192

Mount Eliza Stroke Club: Contact Caulfield Hospital |
S. Australia	Stroke Club, Payenham Rehabilitation Centre, 411 Payenham Rd., Felixtowe, 5070
W. Australia	Stroke Association of W.A., P.O. Box 265, Nedlands, 6009
Tasmania	Tasmania Stroke Club, Speech Pathologist, Douglas Parker Rehabilitation Centre, 31 Tower Rd, New Town, 7008

ACT   The Onward Stroke Club
              C/- The Uniting Church
              9 Denman Street
              Yarralumla ACT 2600
              ph (062) 86 3534

              Belconnen Stroke Club
              C/- Belconnen Churches
              Benjamin Way
              Belconnen ACT 2615
              ph (062) 51 2268

Overseas

New Zealand   Counterstroke New Zealand Inc.
              P.O. Box 2320 Wellington
England   Chest, Heart and Stroke Association, London
U.S.A.   American Heart Association,
              St. Petersburg, Florida
Canada   Stroke Recovery Association,
              Ontario, Canada
South Africa Stroke Club,
              Johannesburg, South Africa
Japan   Stroke Research Club, Faculty of Medicine,
              University of Tsukuba, Ibaraki, Japan 305
Sweden   Stroke-Foreningen: Stockholm
              Sveavagen (Wennergren-Centre) Stockholm,
              Sweden

The following books are available at The Stroke Recovery Centre

A Stroke in the Family   Valerie Eaton Griffith
                            This book shows that the concerted
                            efforts of friends and relatives may
                            help the person who has had a stroke
                            to regain speech and mental capacity
                            and the will to live.
A Time to Speak   Valerie Eaton Griffith
                            Patricia Oetliker

Living After a Stroke / *When Half is Whole*
Prue Oswen
Positive ideas for helping stroke persons at home and in groups.
Diana Law/Barbara Paterson
Lorna Hewson
My recovery from stroke. Valuable for all concerned with management of strokes.

Practical activities
For Stroke Groups
Andrea Miller, LCST
Ruth Coles, LCST
Workbook of activities for group work

Stroke
Janice Walker Dip. O.T. (NZ)
An illustrated booklet.

Living With a Stroke: The Challenge
Case histories reported with a human eye and a sharp pencil.

Stroke — and How I Survived It
Ron Saw
A moving account of life after a stroke.

Stroke — Who Cares?
Pauline Willis
An experience of a stroke person's spouse.

Retraining For the Elderly Disabled
Margaret Mort M.B.E., Dip. O.T., A.S.T.C.
(Croom Helm)
Written for people working in the field of rehabilitation but equally valuable for families of stroke.
Available at major book sellers.

A Motor Relearning Programme for Stroke
Janet H. Carr and Roberta Shepherd

Available at major book sellers.

MORE TITLES FROM COLLINS DOVE

Pills, Potions, People
Liz Byrski

This book attempts to put the drug problem in perspective for the reader who has little or no knowledge of the subject.
A major purpose of the book is to increase understanding of the fact that drug addiction and dependency, although generally viewed as forms of social protest, are, in fact, the extreme results of our present drug taking behaviour, based on habits rooted in conformity and convention. An important theme of the book is that the reasons people use, abuse and become dependent on, or addicted to, drugs are more important than the drugs themselves.
Pills, Potions, People provides a broad overview of drug use and social attitudes towards them; including social, recreational, over the counter and prescription drugs and illegal substances. Other sections deal with individual drugs, both legal and illegal, looking at the history of their use and the ways they are used today.
Liz Byrski is a journalist. She is the author of *Facing Cancer*.

MORE TITLES FROM COLLINS DOVE

Lupus: A Wolf in Sheep's Clothing

Keren Hardy

One of the most difficult problems people may have to face is long term illness - let alone an illness that is difficult to diagnose and that nobody really understands. Sufferers from the disease Systemic Lupus Erythematosus (SLE) are faced with both these problems. Lupus can affect different parts of the body, typically beginning with fatigue and pains in the joints, and travels an unpredictable course of apparent good health one day and incapacity the next.

Keren Hardy was a trainee nurse when she discovered that the vague feeling of ill-health she had suffered for a year was a disease that she had never heard of before. Her experiences with Lupus and her concern for other sufferers made her want to share with them and their families what she had learnt. She explores the cause and course of the disease, the available treatment, side-effects caused by medication, what sort of work a Lupus sufferer can do, and how to cope with the human and physical environment.

Medical practitioners and a psychiatrist have advised on this text, but the authority that is apparent in every word comes from the personal experience of one who has faced with fortitude the changes Lupus has brought into her life, and who will not let it defeat her.

MORE TITLES FROM COLLINS DOVE

In Stillness Conquer Fear
Pauline McKinnon

Fear - many of us encounter it from time to time. How many people are crippled by it because it never leaves their side?
Agoraphobia - the fear of leaving the safety of home - affects more people the we would imagine. All phobias stem from tension, which, sadly, is only to common in our helter-skelter society. Too many of us are unskilled at managing the stresses of our lives, which then leads to an increase in our level of tension.
In finding a solution to her most puzzling problem, Pauline McKinnon reveals much about our human nature, and how fear can invade our lives. After many years of unsuccessful attempts at overcoming agoraphobia, she found her own solution in meditative relaxation.
For those who suffer from agoraphobia, or who know someone who does, this book will bring enlightenment and relief. For those of us who simply have an interest in this particular fear, or have some other fear, it fills a gap in the literature which Pauline herself identified: it is a book which avoids complicated technical issues and language; rather it clearly reflects an intimacy with the problem, and gives reassurance to the sufferer, throughout.
Understanding a problem helps in achieving a solution; this is the great value of this book.

MORE TITLES FROM COLLINS DOVE

Under the Influence
Liz Byrski

Alcoholism is no respecter of persons. The disease cuts across the barriers of age, class, income, sex, race and religion. It can lead to domestic violence, child abuse, emotional and financial deprivation, marriage breakdown and suicide. Everyone in the family is at risk.

Under the Influence examines the experience of children in families where there is an alcoholic parent, families in which each individual is touched by the disruptive affects of drinking.

Through extensive interviews with both teenagers and adults the author examines the ways in which feelings and responses developed in childhood weave through adult lives, leaving a trail of chaos.

Anyone who has lived with a drinking problem, their own or that of anyone close to them, will identify with the stories told here, as will anyone who has experienced a crisis of relationships or personal identity. The ways in which people solve their problems and attempt to establish control over their own lives holds a valuable lesson.

MORE TITLES FROM COLLINS DOVE

Happiness - It's Up To You
Sabine Beecher

This best-selling book, in its third printing, shows you how to master the logical thinking that brings happiness. It shows you don't need success or approval of others for good feelings about yourself.
The message of the book is: When you have learnt to depend on yourself, you will actually get on better with others. Sabine Beecher clearly sets out steps on how to make you feel good about yourself and how to build better relationships.

MORE TITLES FROM COLLINS DOVE

Facing Cancer
Liz Byrski

People with cancer and their families are faced with a bewildering choice of therapies both inside and outside established medicine.
How can people make decisions about appropriate treatment and sort fact from fiction and prejudice from honest concern?
This book provides an information base from which individuals may choose to make further investigation of some options or to discard them.

MORE TITLES FROM COLLINS DOVE

Codependent No More
Melody Beattie

Codependent No More is the record breaking, best-selling book that has enjoyed over 105 weeks on the US best-seller list. It presents an overview of codependence, detailing its characteristics, where the behaviour comes from and how it affects us and those around us.

It offers hope and guidance and discusses several options to controlling behaviour and helps us understand that letting go will set us free. The author herself is a recovering alcoholic and drug dependency counsellor.

MORE TITLES FROM COLLINS DOVE

The Good News Bible

Special Features include:
Large Format
Attractive Jacket
Ideal for School or Personal Use
Features and introduction to each book of the bible
Cross references
600 line illustrations by Annie Villaton
Outline Chart of Bible History
Word list explaining unfamiliar words
Index of important subjects
Colour and black and white maps of biblical places
Includes Deuterocanonical/Apocrypha Books